I0797630

THE ART OF

Disney · PIXAR HOPPERS

Foreword by Pete Docter

Introduction by Daniel Chong

CHRONICLE BOOKS
SAN FRANCISCO

FRONT COVER Daniel López Muñoz, *digital*

BACK COVER Daniel López Muñoz, *digital*

FRONT FLAP John Cody Kim, *pen on paper*

BACK FLAP John Cody Kim, *digital*

ENDSHEETS Daniel López Muñoz, *digital*

PAGE 1 Daniel López Muñoz, *digital*

PAGES 2–3 Valerie Kao, *digital*

THIS SPREAD Daniel López Muñoz, *digital*

Library of Congress Cataloging-in-Publication Data available.

978-1-7972-3707-7

Manufactured in China.

Design by Liam Flanagan.

10 9 8 7 6 5 4 3 2 1

Chronicle Books LLC
680 Second Street
San Francisco, California 94107
www.chroniclebooks.com

SCIENCE
E&M

Foreword

When Daniel Chong first pitched his action-adventure spy thriller film *Hoppers*, I said, "Dam, this idea is gnawsome! There's so much to chew on. Wood you believe I've never heard anything as *un-fur-gettable*?"

Okay, I didn't say any of those things. There's just something about beavers that invites bad puns. Sorry about that.

Beavers are cute. They're also nature's workaholics, tirelessly chewing, constructing, and reshaping their world like tiny, furry architects with an insatiable drive. And they don't just build dams; they build entire ecosystems, making them one of nature's most influential engineers. In a way, they embody the very themes of *Hoppers*—resilience and teamwork. So when Daniel pitched his idea about being able to experience the world from a beaver's point of view, we knew he was onto something truly *lodge-ical*. (Okay, enough. Stopping with the puns.)

But of course, a great idea alone won't build a movie. You can't point a camera at a concept. Someone has to take those concepts and make them into something real. And with animation, you can't just look around at your mom's house and borrow a lamp to put on the set; everything you see on-screen—every tree, every ripple of water, every perfectly gnawed log, even the actors themselves—has to be designed, built, textured, and lit. And that's where the talented folks in this book come in.

Designing for animation isn't just about making things look cool. After all, we don't watch movies just to see things happen; we watch because we want to *feel* something. The images in this book aren't just blueprints for construction—they are the sturdy logs (uh-oh, I'm slipping) that shape whether we feel safe in our cozy den or sense danger lurking downstream. To emotionally evoke whatever the story requires: This is the real job of a film designer.

So as you gnaw through these pages, take a moment to chew over the artistry behind the adventure. This is where *Hoppers* began—not in the final polished frames, but in the raw, dam-bursting creativity that first brought these beavers to life.

(Sorry, blame the beavers.)

Pete Docter, executive producer

LEFT Daniel López Muñoz, *digital* **ABOVE** Daniel Chong, *marker on paper*

Introduction

It started as a pitch called *Penguin Avatar*. The negative feedback I got was that maybe the world didn't need another animated penguin movie. *No problem*, I thought. *I can change that*. Kinda couldn't believe it was just the penguin part that tripped everyone up.

So . . . *Hoppers*? Is this a movie about bunnies? No, it's actually about ~~penguins~~ beavers. I was inspired by those nature documentaries where people put a robotic animal into the wild to spy on animals up close. Some robots are incredibly realistic; other robots are kind of . . . hilariously off. The notion of "hopping" (transferring your brain into a robotic animal) was to me just the next logical step in our weird human attempts to infiltrate the animal world.

For the characters, I remember a few key drawings that informed who would be the stars: a young animal-loving girl tackling some dude for almost stepping on an ant, a group of weird scientists in a secret lab full of janky robots, and a beaver wearing a crown and blissfully smiling into the air.

But what kind of movie is this? A comedy? A drama? An action movie? Espionage thriller? Sci-fi?? Horror?! YES to all. If there's a genre, throw it in. Mix it up. Pull it out, dry it, and run it again. There's probably a movie in there somewhere.

Huge set pieces, landscape vistas, an enormous cast of both humans and animals, massive fire and water effects . . . if there was a technical complexity, this movie had it. All along the way, I kept thinking, *Yeah, but what else can I add?*

I approached this project full of endless ambition to what I thought a Pixar movie could be. In my defense, I had just finished producing a TV show with a small budget, and suddenly I was given the opportunity to make a feature film. This was it—the opportunity to go BIG! RIGHT???

OPPOSITE Melody Cisinski, *digital*

Daniel Chong, *marker on paper*

Daniel Chong, *marker on paper*

Daniel Chong, *marker on paper*

John Cody Kim, *marker on paper*

John Cody Kim, *marker on paper*

This next part is embarrassing. I soon realized I was making a film that was not producible: over three hours long (in animation, we don't get Christopher Nolan run times), way too many ideas, and it didn't make any sense. Oh, and I needed to cut twelve characters to get under budget. This movie was out of control. It was stressful. And I was out of my depth. HELP.

Somehow, the movie got made. Wanna know why? It has less to do with me and more to do with my collaborators. A film of this scale cannot be made alone and requires the help of hundreds of people who are talented and brilliant and care deeply (their beautiful work is featured in this book). I am so grateful to them for embracing this wild movie and wanting it to exist as badly as I did. Everyone worked tirelessly and pushed each other to make the movie better (and embrace the bigness). As our own King George would say, we were all in this together. It was such a relief to know that this huge movie was not mine anymore. It was theirs. Better yet, it was ours.

"It's hard to be mad when you're a part of something big" is what Mabel's grandma tells her at the glade, looking out into nature's expanse and feeling connected.

This movie is big. And I'm lucky I got to be a part of it.

Daniel Chong, director

Daniel Chong, *digital*

John Cody Kim, *digital*

John Cody Kim, *marker on paper*

Daniel Chong, *digital*

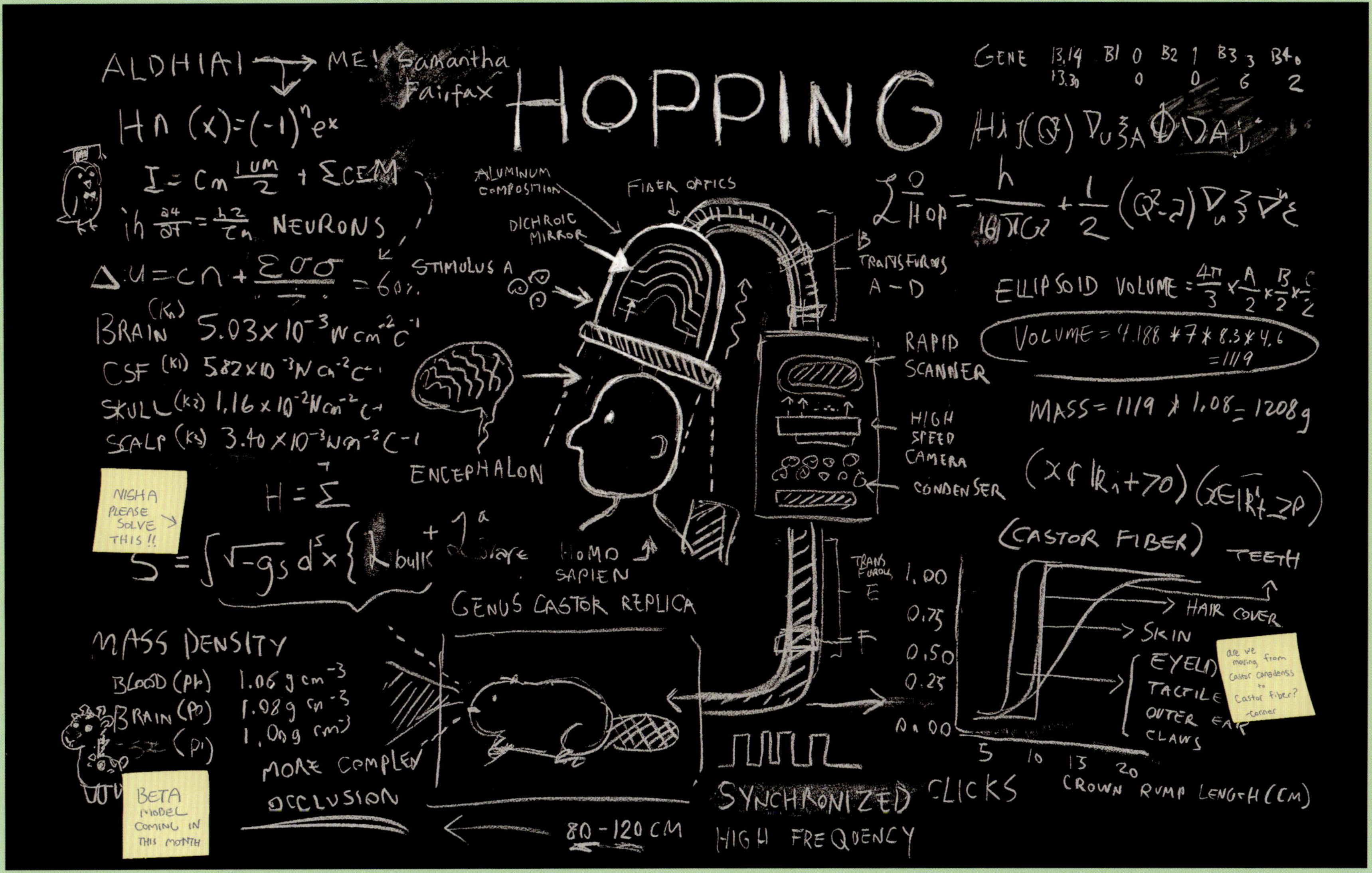

John Cody Kim, *chalk on chalkboard*

John Cody Kim and Dean Kelly, *digital*

Dean Kelly, *digital*

Daniel López Muñoz, *digital*

Madeline Sharafian, *digital*

As a character, Mabel evolved a lot alongside the story of *Hoppers*. We always knew she cared about nature, but we had to hunt to find her "why." The glade was a special place for her and her grandma to bond in, so nature became a sort of proxy for that relationship. We liked the idea of Mabel getting into trouble for standing up for critters just because it wasn't the status quo to care. Mabel is seen as a troublemaker by everyone but her grandmother. So that enduring love is what keeps the fight alive in her.

Margaret Spencer, lead story artist

Daniel Chong, *ink and marker on paper*

Madeline Sharafian, *digital*

Daniel López Muñoz, *digital*

Madeline Sharafian, *digital*

Francesca Fedele, *digital*

Daniel López Muñoz, *digital*

Hye Sung Kim, *digital*

Bryn Imagire, *digital over renders*

I DIDN'T DO ANYTHING

Margaret Spencer, *marker on paper*

Madeline Sharafian, *digital*

Wesley Fuh, *ink and marker on paper*

Anna Scott, *digital*

Daniel López Muñoz, *digital*

Lauren Kawahara, *digital*

Madeline Sharafian, *digital*

Jennifer Nie, *digital*

Anna Scott, *digital*

Margaret Spencer, *marker on paper*

HONK IF HOOOONK!

TOP ROW Jennifer Nie, *digital*

RAMEN
RAMEN
TANAKA
VOTE FOR JERRY

Margaret Spencer, *digital*

Daniel López Muñoz, *digital*

Daniel López Muñoz, *digital*

Anna Scott, *watercolor and digital*

Anna Scott, *digital*

Daniel López Muñoz, *digital*

Daniel López Muñoz, *digital*

Hye Sung Kim, *digital*

Anna Scott, *digital*

Madeline Sharafian, *digital*

BEAVER MABEL

HEAD
- Ears low and small
- little tuft on top (not as essential as cheeks)

FACE
- scruffy cheeks!
- angry little brows

even from far away, the scruff helps identify

- neutral mouth shows teeth (upside down triangle can be enough)

TONE
- Heart-shaped cheek/belly patch
- lighter than King G

BODY
- small front paws
- big paddle-like feet
- not a lot of "leg" →

even when stretched, mostly foot

TAIL
- Big! Try to cheat to show it in her silhouette
- some texture

Yogin and Madeline Sharafian, *digital*

Yogin, *digital*

Anna Scott, *digital*

Yogin, *digital*

Victor Navone, *digital*

Daniel López Muñoz, *digital*

Bryn Imagire, *photography*

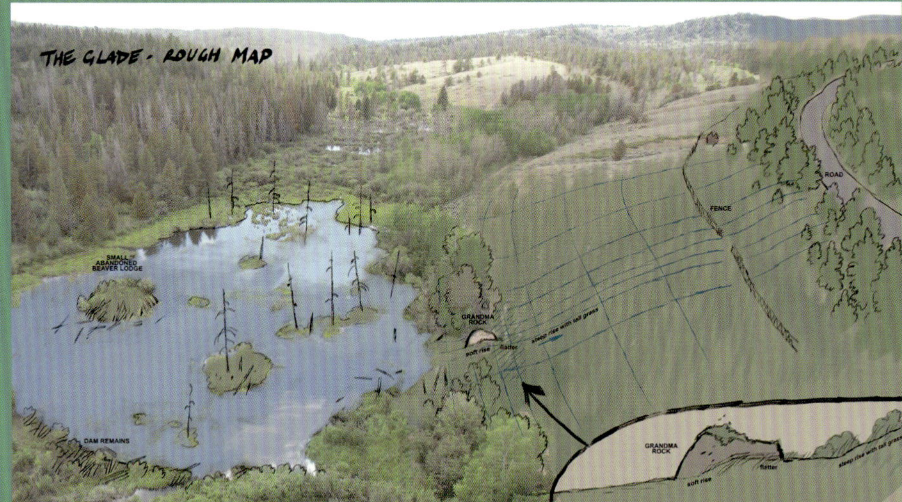

Daniel López Muñoz, *digital*

Bryn Imagire, *photography*

Going on the research trip was amazing; it really inspired a lot of the art we did. It wasn't just the dams and lodges that stuck out, but the smaller details, too—like little tunnels and pathways carved through willow bushes and grasses, new-cut and old-cut trees, water lines on rocks from old ponds after beavers moved on. We got to visit a beaver pond in an area that had fire damage, and seeing the contrast between burnt mountainsides and green new growth around the pond was a stark example of just how much the landscape changes when a beaver moves in. It's a very specific environment that would have been hard to capture without seeing it in person. Plus, seeing a beaver eat a stick up close was pretty cool, too.

Anna Scott, character art director and lead drawover artist

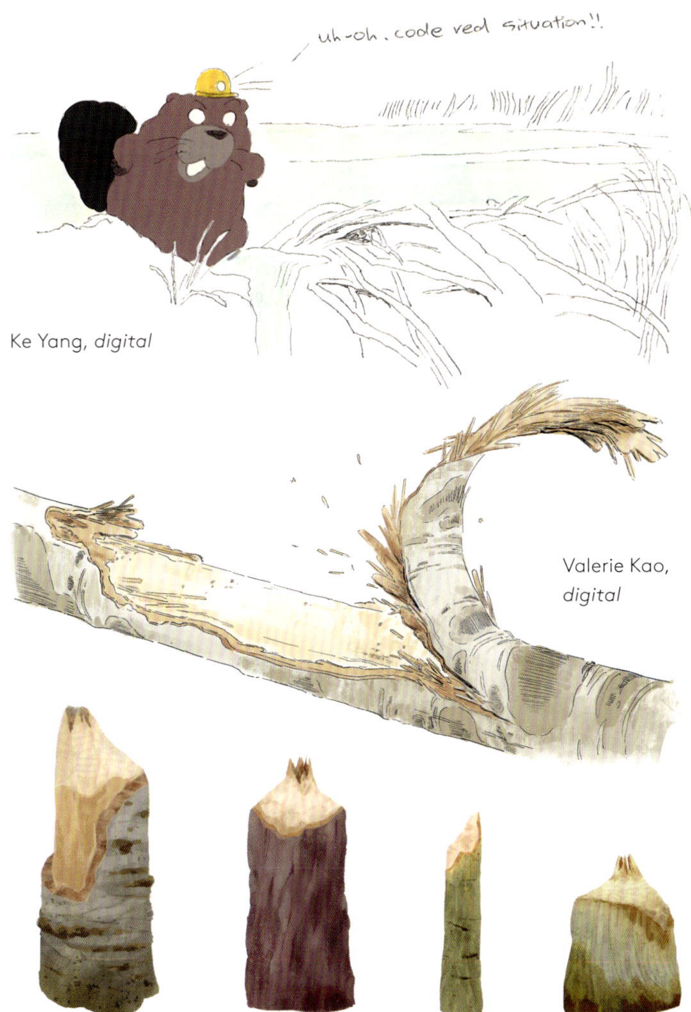

Ke Yang, *digital*

Valerie Kao, *digital*

Lauren Kawahara and Daniel Holland, *digital*

WATER SLIDE!

Ke Yang, *digital*

Carlos Felipe Léon and Daniel López Muñoz, *digital*

Kerascoët, *pencil and watercolor on paper*

Valerie Kao, *digital*

Valerie Kao, *digital*

Ralph Eggleston, *digital*

Bryn Imagire, *paper, clay, and wire,* and Deborah Coleman, *photography*

Anna Scott, *digital*

Philip Metschan, *digital*

Bert Berry, *digital*

Ke Yang, *digital*

Anna Scott, *digital*

RIGHT Kaleb Rice (3D models) and Carlos Felipe Léon (painting), *digital*

MABEL'S MEMORIES

Wesley Fuh, Margaret Spencer, and Hannah Roman, *digital*

Nature's ability to connect and heal has always been a core element of the film . . . and some version of this scene has been a part of Mabel's story since the very first screening. We wanted the audience to experience firsthand the peace and sense of purpose that the glade and its animal inhabitants brought her, and how deeply connected she felt to her grandmother there. Mabel is such an intense and, at times, chaotic character, and the glade and Grandma gave her a space to not only calm and center herself but also channel her fiery temperament for good. We tried putting this scene in different parts of the film, but ultimately, we felt that placing it in the front helped the audience connect more deeply with our protagonist. **Hannah Roman, lead story artist**

Valerie Kao, *digital*

Daniel Holland (drawing) and Jonathan Chen (painting), *digital*

Ke Yang, *digital*

Anna Scott, *digital*

Wesley Fuh, *marker on paper*

Ke Yang, *digital*

Anna Scott, *digital*

Valerie Kao, *digital*

Ke Yang, *digital*

Wesley Fuh, *marker on paper*

Hye Sung Kim, *digital*

Daniel López Muñoz, *digital*

Daniel López Muñoz, *digital*

John Cody Kim, *marker on paper*

SAVE THE DAM

Margaret Spencer, Hannah Roman, Nira Liu, and Michael Fong, *digital*

This scene likely passed through the hands of every story artist on the team at some point and went through countless iterations to get just right. While plot-wise it appears to be a simple setup for the present-day threat to the glade, there's much more at play. Above all, this is a scene about power dynamics and character. It introduces an adult Mabel and her formidable antagonist, Mayor Jerry, who we need the audience to simultaneously hate *and* love spending time with. It also has to set the stage for the film's central conflict while prodding the audience to sympathize, judge, laugh, and enjoy the ride. **Hannah Roman, lead story artist**

Hye Sung Kim, *digital*

Kyle Jones, *digital*

John Cody Kim, *pen on paper*

John Cody Kim, *digital*

John Cody Kim, *marker on paper*

Jacy Zuckerbrow, *digital*

Kyle Jones and Hye Sung Kim, *digital*

Daniel López Muñoz, *digital*

Ke Yang, *digital*

Ke Yang, *digital*

Hye Sung Kim and Kaleb Rice, *digital*

DOOR TO DOOR

Margaret Spencer, *digital*

These boards are from a sequence called "Door to Door"; the sequence was created to show Mabel's exhausting failure to save the glade the "right" way . . . by politely asking for signatures on a petition! We knew the main idea behind this scene—when Mabel plays by the rules, she loses. We came up with a ton of gags, and really found the rhythm of the scene in editorial, thanks to some really fun acting choices. **Margaret Spencer, lead story artist**

Carlos Felipe Léon and Daniel Holland, *digital*

Daniel López Muñoz, *digital*

Anna Scott, *digital*

Carlos Felipe Léon and Daniel Holland, *digital*

Valerie Kao, *digital*

Valerie Kao, *digital*

Daniel Holland, *matte board, acrylic sheets, and acrylic paint*

Daniel Holland (drawing) and Lauren Kawahara, *digital*

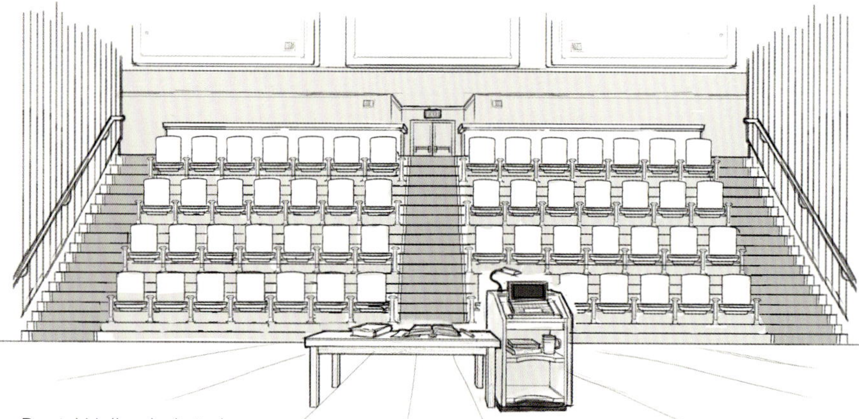

Daniel Holland, *digital*

Hye Sung Kim and Daniel Holland, *digital*

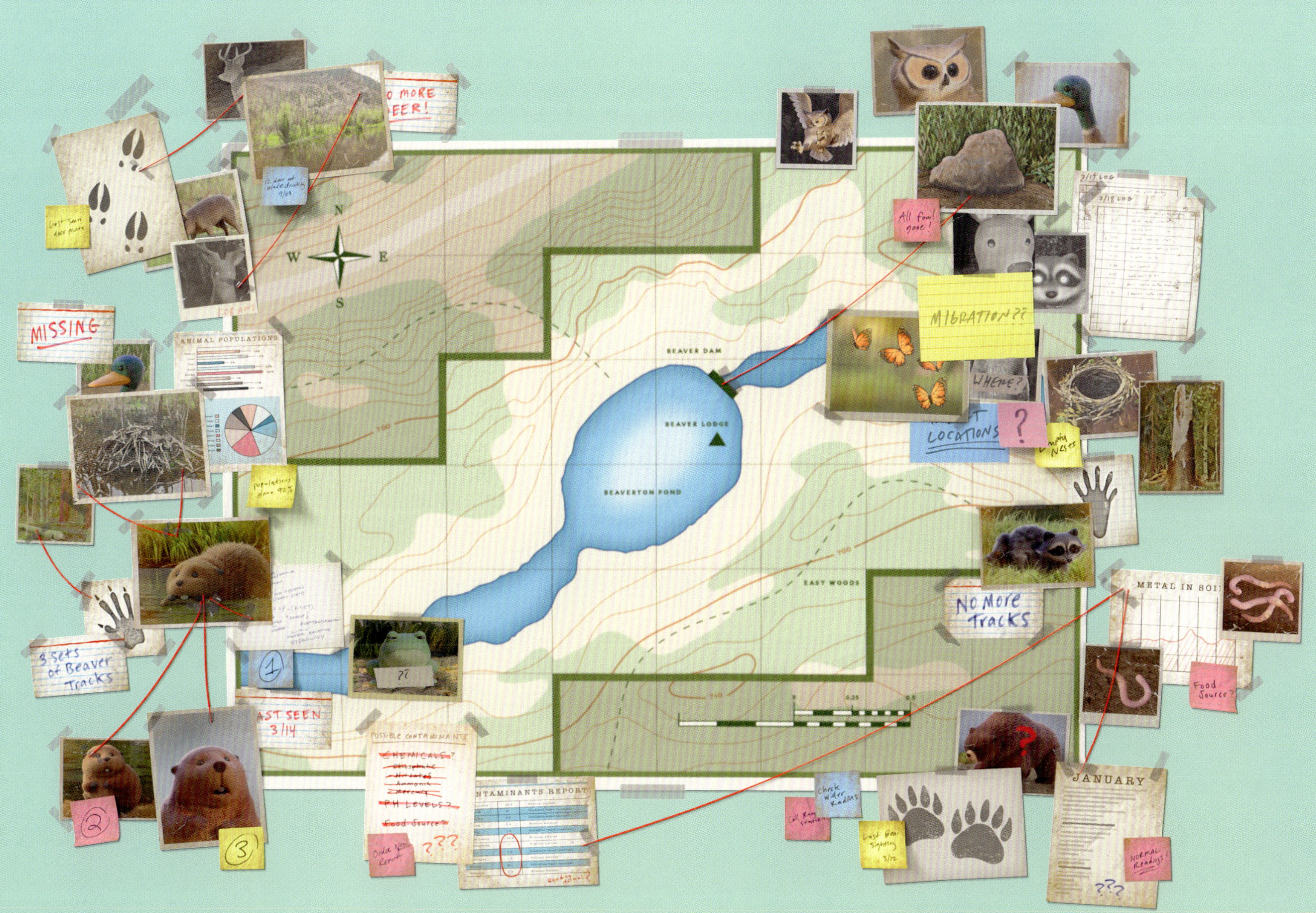

Kyle Jones and Bert Berry, *digital*

Daniel López Muñoz, *digital*

Madeline Sharafian, *digital*

Daniel López Muñoz, *digital*

Anna Scott, *digital*

Daniel López Muñoz (character design) and Anna Scott, *digital*

Margaret Spencer, *marker on paper*

John Cody Kim, *marker on paper*

Margaret Spencer, *digital*

Daniel López Muñoz, *digital*

Hye Sung Kim, *digital*

Hye Sung Kim, *digital*

Airi Pan, *digital*

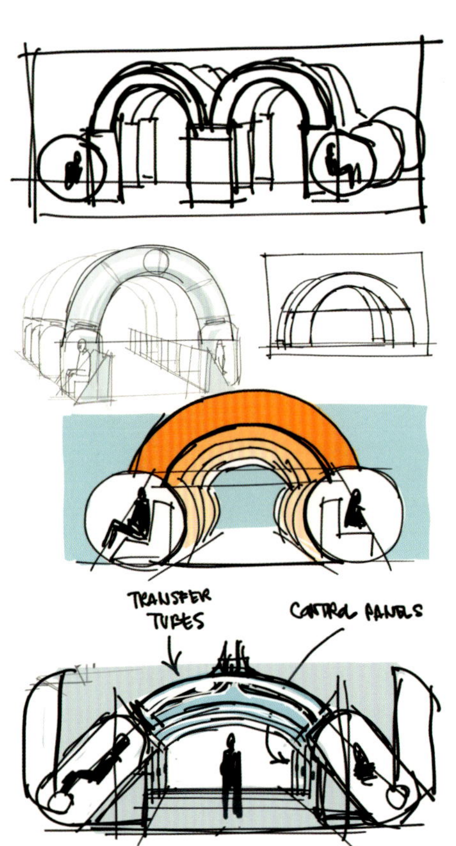

Jay Shuster, *digital*

Jay Shuster, *digital*

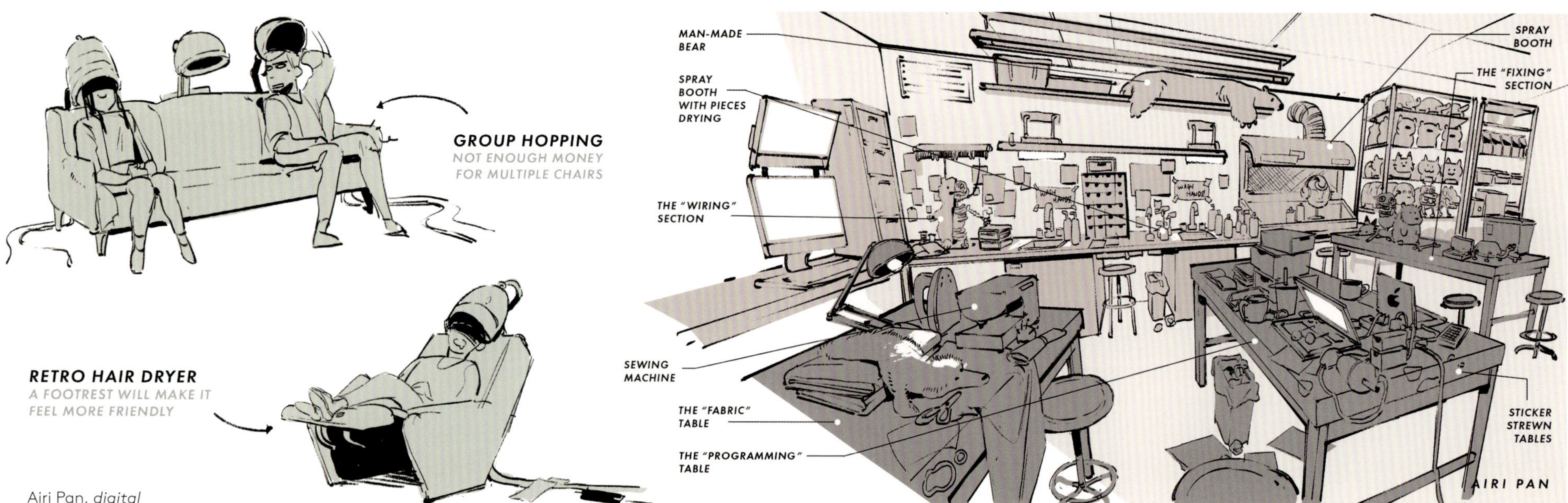

Airi Pan, *digital*

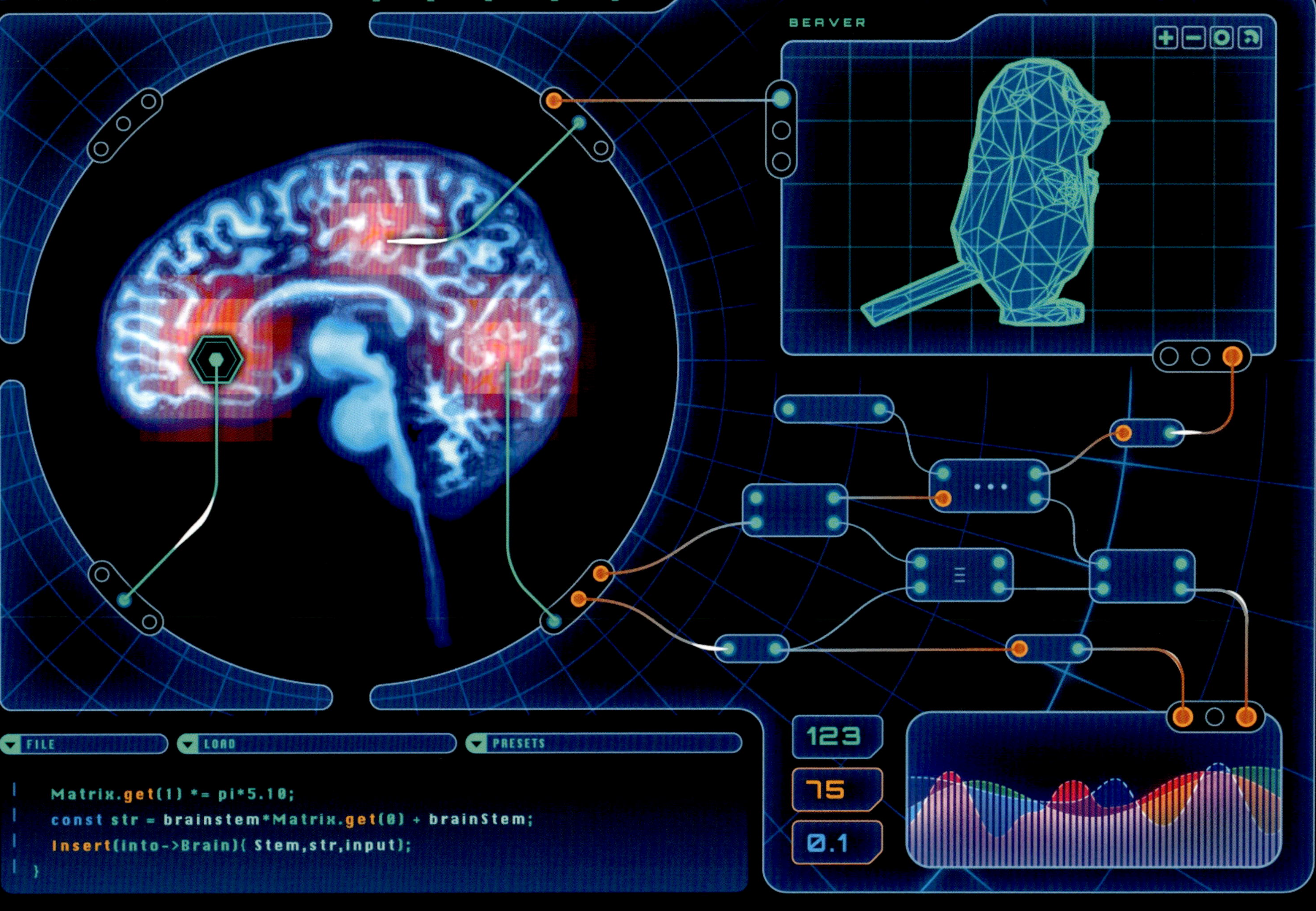

Kyle Jones, *digital*

HOPPER'S LAB

Sylvain Marc, *digital*

John Cody Kim, *digital*

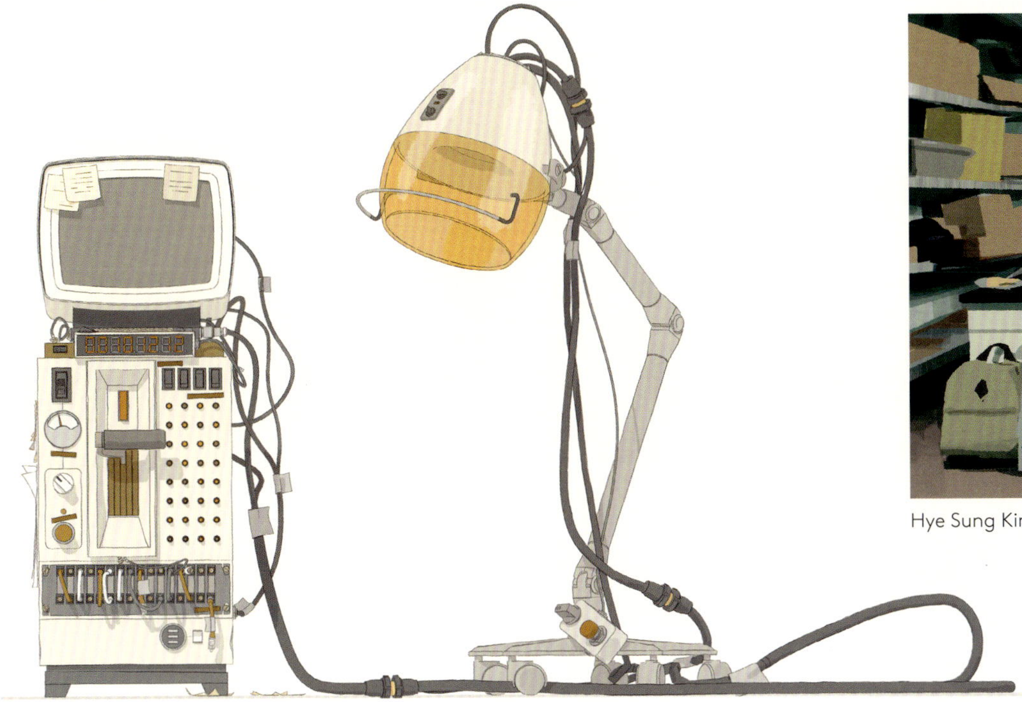

Hye Sung Kim, *digital*

Daniel López Muñoz, *digital*

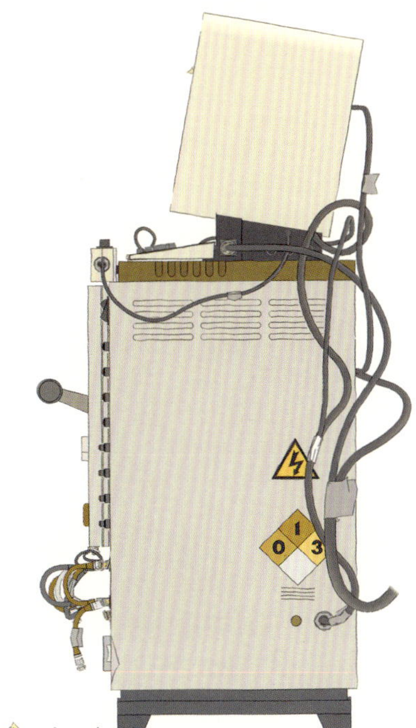

Daniel López Muñoz, *digital*

Lauren Kawahara and Daniel López Muñoz, *digital*

John Cody Kim and Annlyn Huang (designs) and Bryn Imagire, *digital*

EARLY PROTOTYPES HOP BEAVERS

UGH... GUYS.
I SEEM TO BE
STUCK AND CAN'T
HOP OUT..

John Cody Kim, *marker on paper*

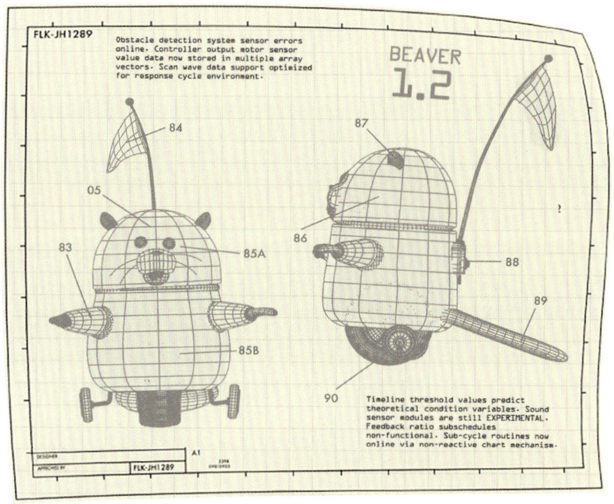

MUST BE
HIDDEN BEHIND
BUSHES AT ALL
TIMES

THERES WIRE
THATS ATTACHED TO HOP MACHINE

WOW,
I CAN'T SEEM
TO GRAB
ANYTHING WITH
THESE CLAWS

FLK-JH1289

Obstacle detection system sensor errors online. Controller output motor sensor value data now stored in multiple array vectors. Scan wave data support optimized for response cycle environment.

BEAVER
1.2

Timeline threshold values predict theoretical condition variables. Sound sensor modules are still EXPERIMENTAL. Feedback ratio subschedules non-functional. Sub-cycle routines now online via non-reactive chart mechanism.

Bert Berry, *digital*

Carlos Felipe Léon and Annlyn Huang, *digital*

HOPPERS' LAB

John Cody Kim and Dean Kelly, *digital*

Figuring out how hopping worked was a topic of endless discussion and exploration. Not that we actually had to make total sense of it (thankfully). But are they putting human minds into actual animals? Are they turning themselves into animals? Are they genetically creating fake animals to go into? We settled on putting your mind into a robot because it just felt the weirdest—and also maybe the least disturbing.

And, yes, I did read the *Animorphs* beaver book, and, no, it did not help. **Daniel Chong, director**

Anna Scott, *digital*

Margaret Spencer, *digital*

Ke Yang, *digital*

Anna Scott, *digital*

Yogin, *digital*

Daniel López Muñoz, *digital*

Ke Yang, *digital*

Daniel López Muñoz, *digital*

Ke Yang, *digital*

Maria Yi, *digital*

Yogin, *digital*

Carlos Felipe Léon and Kaleb Rice, *digital*

Valerie Kao and Daniel López Muñoz, *digital*

John Cody Kim, *ink on lined paper*

Lorenzo Fresta, *digital*

Daniel Chong, *digital*

Anna Scott, *digital*

John Cody Kim, *ink on paper*

John Cody Kim, *ink on paper*

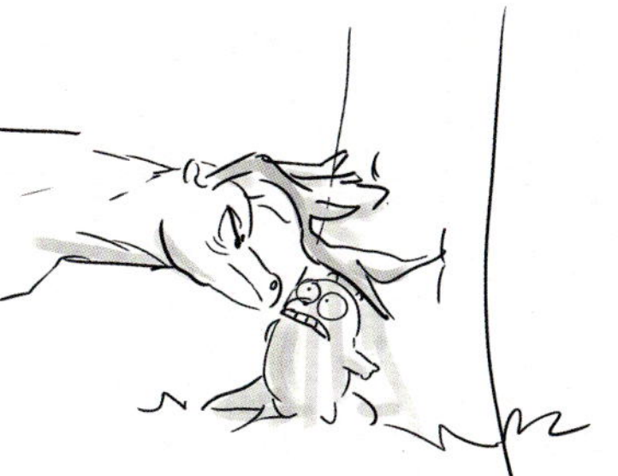

Daniel Chong, *ink on paper*

Margaret Spencer, *ink on paper*

Hye Sung Kim, *digital*

Anna Scott, *digital*

Ke Yang, *digital*

Anna Scott, *digital*

Margaret Spencer, *ink on paper*

Jennifer Nie and Anna Scott, *digital*

Annlyn Huang, *digital*

Anna Scott, *watercolor and digital*

Hye Sung Kim, *digital*

Kaleb Rice, *digital*

Ke Yang, *digital*

Daniel Chong, *digital*

Lauren Kawahara, *digital*

Annlyn Huang, *digital*

Yogin, *digital*

Anna Scott, *digital*

Daniel Chong, *digital*

Hye Sung Kim, *digital*

Anna Scott, *digital*

Valerie Kao, *digital*

Anna Scott, *digital*

Yogin, *digital*

Yogin, *digital*

Anna Scott, *digital*

Anna Scott, *digital*

Laura Phillips and Kaleb Rice, *digital*

BEAR INTERVENTION

Nicolle Castro, *digital*

In this sequence, Mabel has her first in-depth encounter with the animal world, and it definitely doesn't go as she expected! Animating furry characters is always a challenge, especially when they're climbing (and chomping) all over each other, and drenching them in a stream raises the technical bar even higher. In true Pond Rules fashion, our technical teams collaborated closely to bring this sequence to the screen, showcasing the film's tone and themes through the beautiful natural environment, the charm and appeal of the characters, and the comic absurdity of their predicament. **Beth Albright, visual effects supervisor**

I think this was the first time I had to board animal characters, which ended up being really fun, especially with these chonky sets of animals! Although I had to keep in mind real animal behaviors, and in this case how a bear will catch its prey, I also took some creative liberties, like how Ellen eats Loaf like a sandwich—which seems appropriate, given his name! **Nicolle Castro, story artist**

Anna Scott, *digital*

Margaret Spencer, *ink on paper*

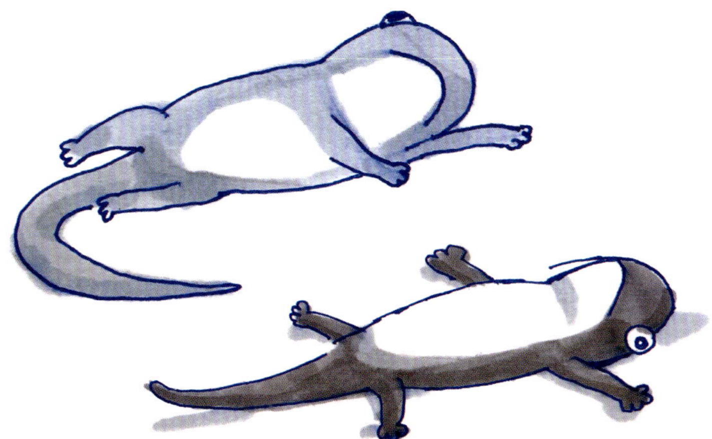

Madeline Sharafian, *ink and marker on paper*

Kerascoët, *digital*

Geek out on lodge construction together, King George is very patient with all her questions (even if no one else is)

Madeline Sharafian, *digital*

Daniel López Muñoz, *digital*

Kerascoët, *digital*

John Cody Kim, *digital*

Sylvain Marc, *digital*

Sylvain Marc and Bryn Imagire, *digital*

Bryn Imagire, *photography*

Kerascoët, *pencil on paper*

Carlos Felipe León, *digital*

Very early on, we made a practical model of a beaver lodge and dam. I wanted to experiment with capturing the appeal of a miniature model but also get the essence of what it feels like to be outside in nature.

Bryn Imagire, production designer

OPPOSITE Jerome Ranft, Meghan Sasaki, Gaston Ugarte, and Bryn Imagire, *resin, foam, wire, and natural materials,* and Deborah Coleman, *photography*

Hye Sung Kim, *digital*

Anna Scott, *digital*

one - and two -
and three

Daniel Chong, *ink on paper*

- LESSONS UNDER THE TREE -

Ke Yang, *digital*

WORKOUT

Daniel Chong, John Cody Kim, and Wesley Fuh, *digital*

Hoppers provided many opportunities for us to work in a number of different cinematic styles. We start this scene by building up tension, kind of like a horror movie, using creeping camera movements, ominous shadows, and shots that put us in Mabel's perspective by not revealing any information to the audience that Mabel doesn't also know. Once King George makes his dramatic entrance and starts exercising, we immediately switch to a more dynamic visual style reflecting the goofiness of what we're witnessing. Big contrasts like this are part of the film's cinematic language. **Jeremy Lasky, director of photography**

Hye Sung Kim and Kaleb Rice, *digital*

Wesley Fuh, *digital*

Yogin, *digital*

Anna Scott, *watercolor and digital*

John Cody Kim, *digital*

John Cody Kim, *digital*

- crown! simple 3 points, or can add depth w/black

FACE

- smoother cheeks than Mabel (still round!)
- eyebags to indicate age
- butt-chin
- alert, happy neutral expression

- more foot than leg even when stretched

- cutie-pie round boy - tubby folds when he moves

- larger than Mabel

Yogin and Madeline Sharafian, *digital*

Madeline Sharafian, *digital*

Madeline Sharafian, *ink and marker on paper*

Madeline Sharafian, *digital*

Anna Scott, *digital*

Daniel Chong, *digital*

Daniel Chong, *digital*

John Cody Kim, *ink on paper*

Yogin, *digital*

Kaleb Rice, *digital*

Valerie Kao, *digital*

Wesley Fuh, *digital*

When I first started on this scene, none of it existed in the script! I drew up a smattering of funny Pond Rules King George would invent and pitched this to the team. These were then turned into script pages by our writer, Jesse Andrews, and handed back to me to storyboard! I felt like a beaver bringing those first sticks of an idea to eventually build into a full dam scene.

Wesley Fuh, story artist

John Cody Kim, *digital*

Daniel Chong, *digital*

Wesley Fuh, *digital*

Daniel Chong, *digital*

Hye Sung Kim, *digital*

Lauren Kawahara and Maria Yi, *digital*

Asha Farmer, *digital*

Maria Yi, *digital*

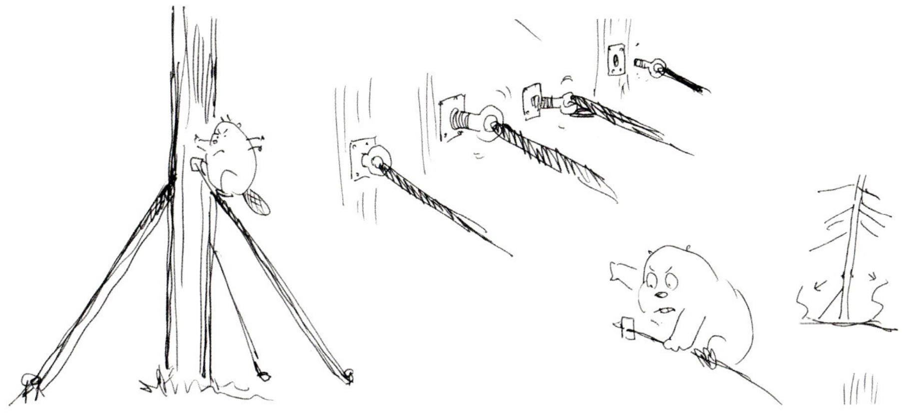

John Cody Kim, *digital*

Hye Sung Kim, *digital*

Maria Yi, *digital*

Anna Scott, *digital*

A DAY'S HARD WORK

"AND THIS IS WHERE WE CHILL!"

Lorenzo Fresta, *digital*

implemented "snack time" into a busy beaver's schedule

Wesley Fuh, *digital*

TEAM WORK

Ke Yang, *digital*

Margaret Spencer, *digital*

John Cody Kim, *digital*

BEAVER PARTY

John Cody Kim and Vanessa Guvele, *digital*

After Daniel pitched me the idea for this scene, I went on a jog while listening to "Working for the Weekend" by Loverboy on repeat. I imagined what it would be like to see a bunch of beavers building a dam together to the beat of the song. I really wanted to capture the upbeat energy and emphasize how much fun they are having while working as a team. During later iterations, we had Mabel participate in building the dam to keep this scene centered around her and help the viewers experience the community that Mabel can feel she truly belongs to. **John Cody Kim, story supervisor**

Having the music for "Beaver Party" chosen so early in the production had a surprising impact on the visual style for *Hoppers*. The glitz, gloss, and vibes of an early '80s MTV hit inspired us to draw influences from the commercial cinematography of the era. Even more surprising was discovering Loverboy on my year-end recap playlist.
Ian Megibben, director of photography

Valerie Kao, *digital*

Daniel Chong, *digital*

Daniel Chong, *digital*

Margaret Spencer, *digital*

Wesley Fuh, *digital*

Wesley Fuh, *digital*

Daniel López Muñoz, *digital*

Lorenzo Fresta, *digital*

Hye Sung Kim, *digital*

Madeline Sharafian, *digital*

John Cody Kim, *digital*

Wesley Fuh, *ink on paper*

KINGS' ARRIVAL

John Cody Kim and Vanessa Guvele, *digital*

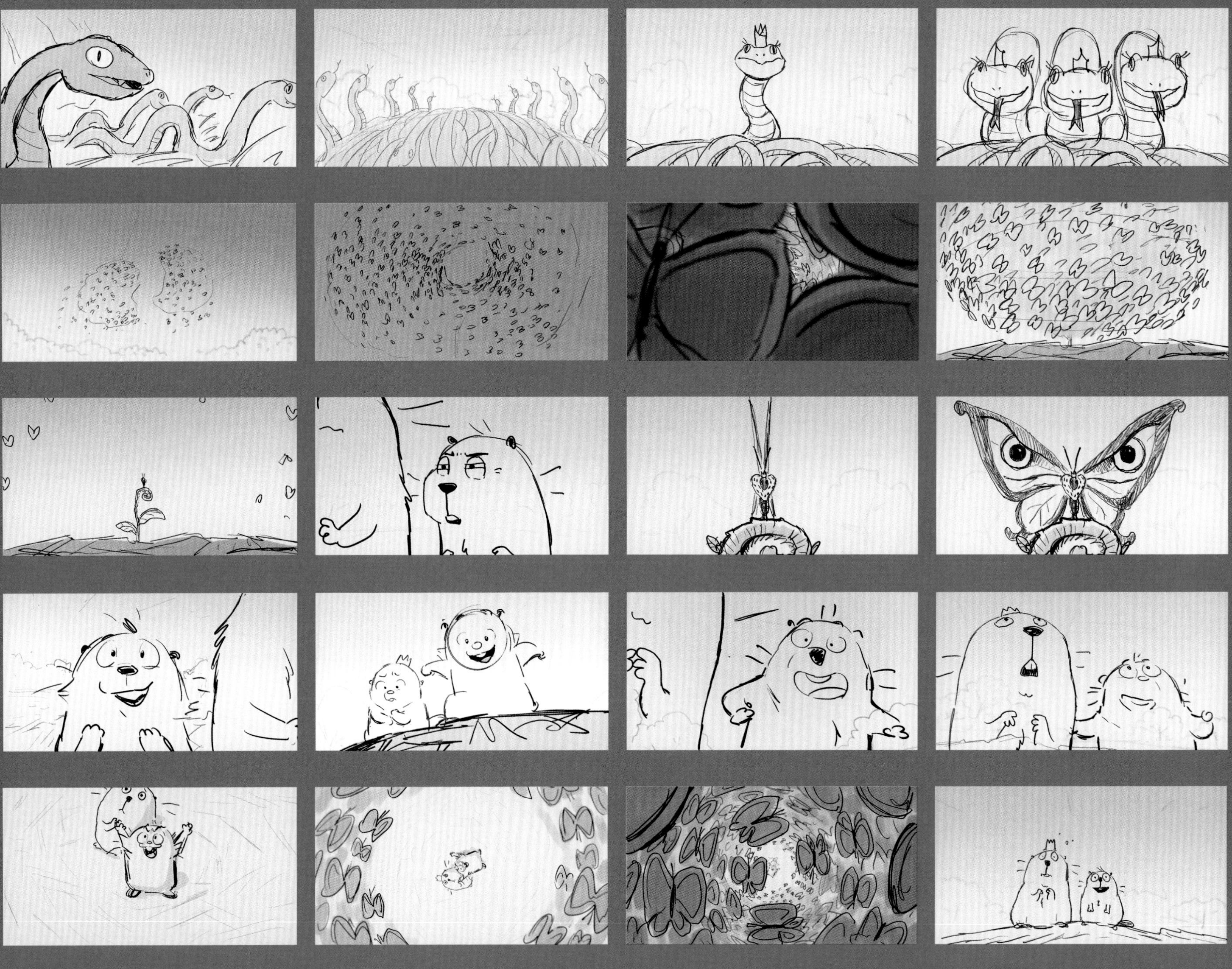

MAMMALS

- chosen as king for his ability to bring the other mammals together
- optimistic
- loves to agree w/others + often encourages conversation

REPTILES

- rattlesnakes have a fun extra emoting tool
- she + her cool snake girlfriends - love to party w/maraca tails
- whenever a cloud passes over, she starts to slur her words (cold-blooded side effect)
- has a high human death bodycount

AMPHIBIANS

- barely moves
- others have to keep checking if he's alive
- poke him w/a stick + he squeals though
- can't seem to stop eyeing king Butterfly
- motivation is on the low side
- pessimistic

BIRDS

- geese are def king of all birds
- intimidation factor: hissing, honking flapping
- already a well-established terrorist of humanity + very proud of it
- always suggests attacks be in a "V" formation

FISH

- a little impotent
- talks a big game but can't really back it up too much
- tries to bring up her friends the sharks as much as possible
- constantly has to dip down into water, misses part of the convo + has to ask what she missed

INSECTS

- "we are many. You are few."
- bugs technically have the majority on Earth
- extremely serious
- possibly violent

Madeline Sharafian, *digital*

John Cody Kim, *ink on paper*

Daniel Chong, *digital*

Wesley Fuh, *digital*

Margaret Spencer, *digital*

Daniel López Muñoz, *digital*

INSIDE the LODGE!

Foyer - smallest room

Some sort of "towel" stack

sorting room

human stuff

throne ~~nook~~ zone

council room

council table

snack sticks!

toilet exit

by the line "backstory" KG is on the throne

open space in front is for the delivery of human goods

← more organically carved-out throne?

Foyer

sorting room

council room

throne zone is its own nook off of the council room

potential staging for unplugged-Mabel

Daniel and I liked the idea that the animal council was made up of species that are found in other countries to broaden the scope of our world. It also gave us the opportunity to use interesting colors for them to contrast with the earthy tones of our location inspirations: Colorado and the Pacific Northwest.

Bryn Imagire, production designer

THIS PAGE Madeline Sharafian, *digital*

Sylvain Marc, *digital*

Hye Sung Kim, *digital*

Yogin, *digital*

Yogin, *digital*

Anna Scott, *digital*

Laura Phillips and Kaleb Rice, *digital*

Kerascoët, *digital*

Kerascoët, *digital*

Madeline Sharafian, *digital*

Yogin, *digital*

Hye Sung Kim, *digital*

Kerascoët, *digital*

Yogin, *digital*

Yogin, *digital*

Laura Phillips and Kaleb Rice, *digital*

Hye Sung Kim, *digital*

Yogin, *digital*

Carlos Felipe Léon and Kaleb Rice, *digital*

Added curling hair at the back of the head. and eyelashes.

look down on her, can see her mouth, and her eyes are more sideways than the prince's.

The wings have crown-shaped motifs.

Yogin

Treating hair

THIS PAGE

Yogin, *digital*

Anna Scott, *digital*

Yogin, *digital*

Carlos Felipe Léon and Kaleb Rice, *digital*

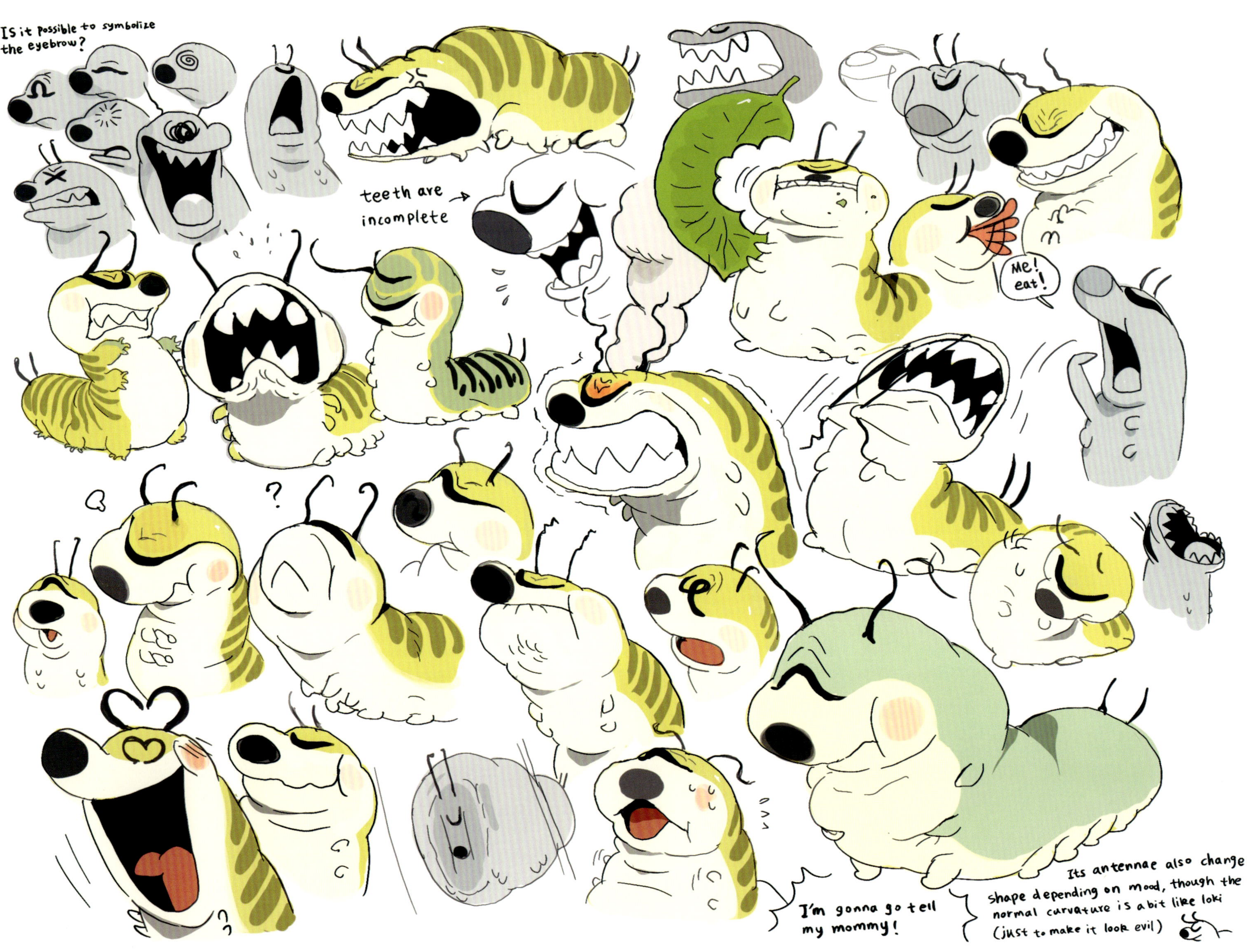

Yogin, *digital*

Hye Sung Kim, *digital*

Carlos Felipe Léon and Kaleb Rice, *digital*

Daniel Chong, *photography*

John Cody Kim, *photography*

During our research trip to Yellowstone, our guide, George Bumann, knew of an abandoned beaver lodge. We were able to experience it firsthand. We squeezed inside through the narrow opening of one of the many entrances and marveled at the amazing construction of mud, sticks, branches, and grasses. It felt so comfortable and homey inside!

Bryn Imagire, production designer

Philip Metschan, *digital*

John Cody Kim, *ink on paper*

Daniel Holland, *digital*

Daniel Holland, *craft foam and acrylic paint*

Daniel Holland, *craft foam and natural materials*

THE COUNCIL

Magaret Spencer, Michael Fong, and John Cody Kim, *digital*

As the tensions rise in the council scene, the situation escalates beyond Mabel's control. When the queen confronts Mabel, it was easy to channel the panic of when a bug flies in your face. The accidental swatting and then wiping of hands was a fun opportunity to show Mabel doing a subconsciously human action that the animal kingdom is shocked and appalled by. **Michael Fong, story artist**

Anna Scott, *digital*

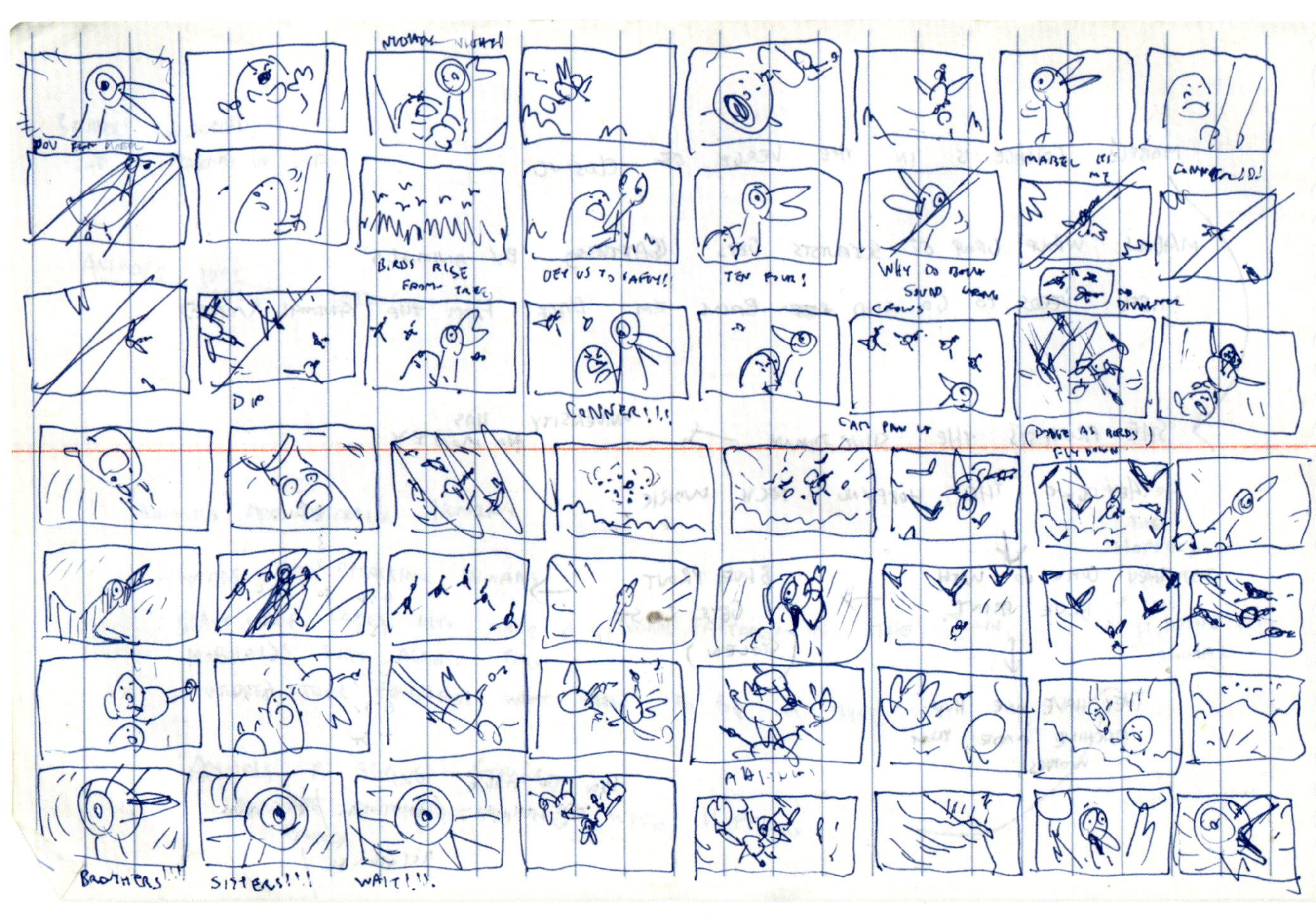

John Cody Kim, *ink on lined paper*

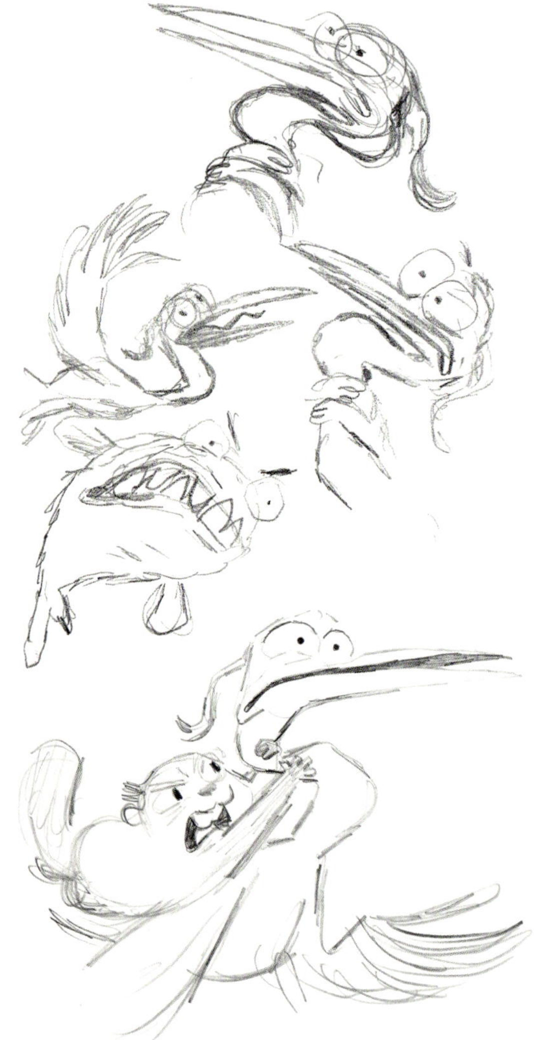

Rob Thompson, *pencil on paper*

Madeline Sharafian, *digital*

Daniel Chong, *digital*

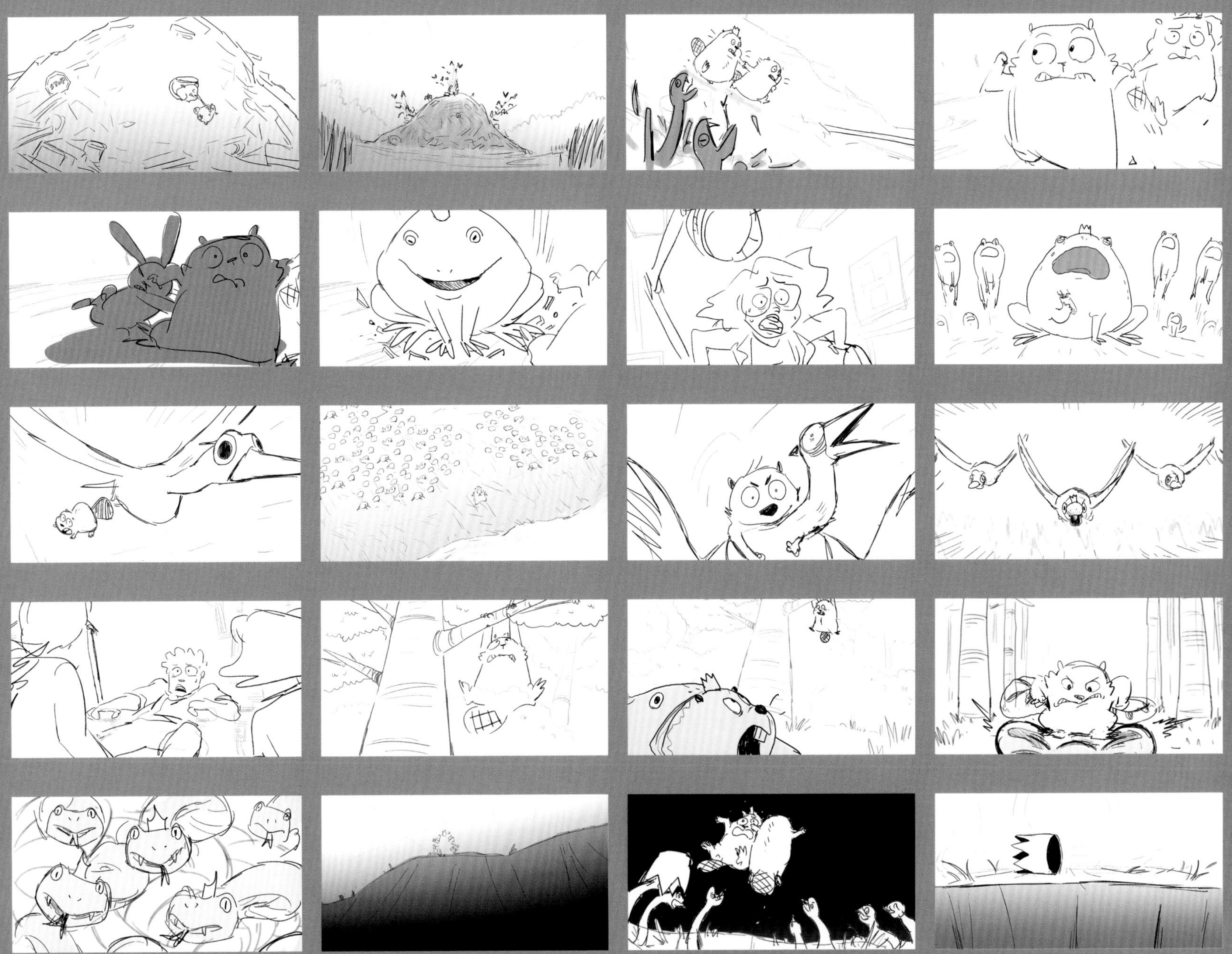

ESCAPE THE LODGE

John Cody Kim and
Michael Fong, *digital*

Wow. This sequence. Once upon a time it was more than double its length. It had everything and the kitchen sink, literally. Maybe it was a bathtub? I swear there was some sort of plumbing fixture enmeshed in that lodge . . . The scene was chock-full of super-fun obstacles and dangers for Mabel and George to deal with. But, when we watched the sequence with the entire movie, it was just too much action. So we had to be ruthless. I removed piranhas, George getting stuck in a hole, and Nisha fighting a cadre of frogs as well as who knows what else to get it down to fighting weight. **Axel Geddes, lead editor**

Daniel López Muñoz, *digital*

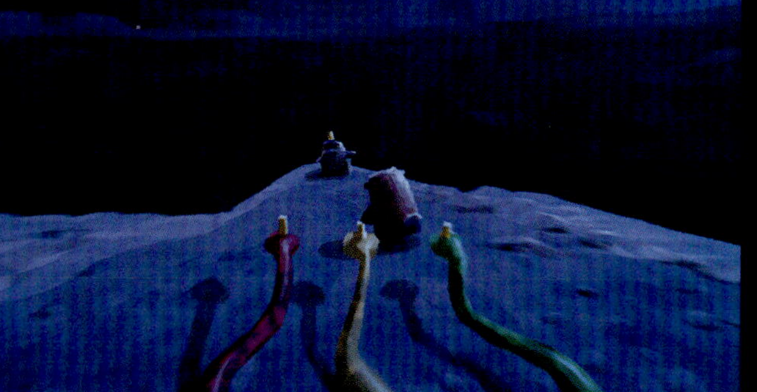

Hye Sung Kim, *digital*

Hye Sung Kim, *digital*

Louie Zong, *digital*

Carlos Felipe Léon and Daniel López Muñoz, *digital*

Valerie Kao, *digital*

John Cody Kim, *ink on paper*

Hye Sung Kim, *digital*

Victor Navone, *digital*

Hye Sung Kim, *digital*

JERRY'S BIG DAY

Margaret Spencer, *digital*

The scene "Jerry's Big Day" was my favorite scene to storyboard. There was no script. The task was to tee up what will be Jerry's very *bad* day. The funniest way to do that, of course, is to show him sitting at the top of the world; everyone loves him, from his neighbors to his mother. It was also our chance to humanize this guy a little bit. We've only seen him from Mabel's point of view—but hey, he's only human! **Margaret Spencer, lead story artist**

Daniel López Muñoz, *digital*

Hye Sung Kim, *digital*

DON'T TURN AROUND

John Cody Kim (storyboards) and Andy Jimenez (emoji), *digital*

Story artists would often huddle in a room, bounce ideas around, draw doodles, and look up reference materials together. After countless drawings of Mayor Jerry in twisted scenarios piling up in the writing room, we came up with "Don't Turn Around." There's something inherently funny about a full-grown man trapped in his own car getting interrogated by a bunch of cuddly animals via text-to-speech on a phone! **John Cody Kim, story supervisor**

DRIVE NOW.
TEXT TO
ANIMALS & NATURE
TEXT TO S

Valerie Kao, *digital*

Carlos Felipe Léon, *digital*

Hye Sung Kim, *digital*

Hye Sung Kim, *digital*

Valerie Kao, *digital*

John Cody Kim, *ink on paper*

John Cody Kim, *digital*

Valerie Kao, *digital*

Anna Scott, *digital*

Anna Scott, *digital*

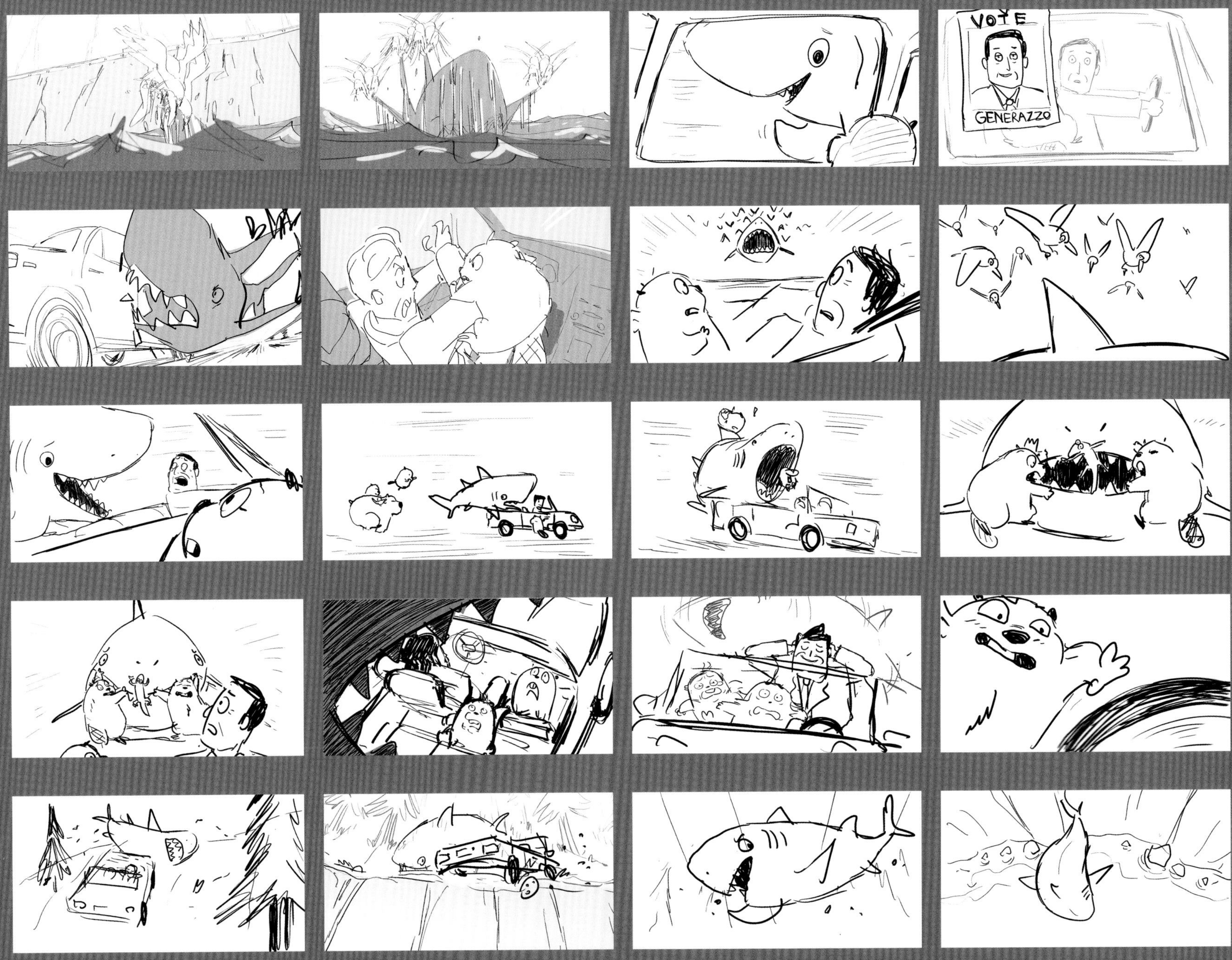

JERRY VS. SHARK

Michael Fong and
John Cody Kim, *digital*

Ah, yes, birds carrying a shark? Pfft! Don't question it; we have animals wearing crowns and a human robot controlled by a bug! We are fully committed here, with some wild ideas! But still . . . when we storyboarded this chase scene, I think many of our reactions were "there's no way this is making it into the movie." And here we are: Sometimes the wildest ideas will make it through all the way to the end and become some of our favorites! **John Cody Kim, story supervisor**

Hye Sung Kim, *digital*

John Cody Kim, *digital*

Margaret Spencer, *digital*

John Cody Kim, *ink on paper*

John Cody Kim, *ink on paper*

Margaret Spencer, *ink on paper*

Margaret Spencer, *ink on paper*

Margaret Spencer, *ink on paper*

John Cody Kim, *ink on paper*

Yogin, *digital*

John Cody Kim, *digital*

Daniel López Muñoz, *digital*

Daniel Chong, *digital*

Yogin, *digital*

Carlos Felipe Léon, *digital*

John Cody Kim, *ink on paper*

John Cody Kim, *digital*

Margaret Spencer, *digital*

Rob Thompson, *pencil on paper*

Rob Thompson, *pencil on paper*

Hye Sung Kim, *digital*

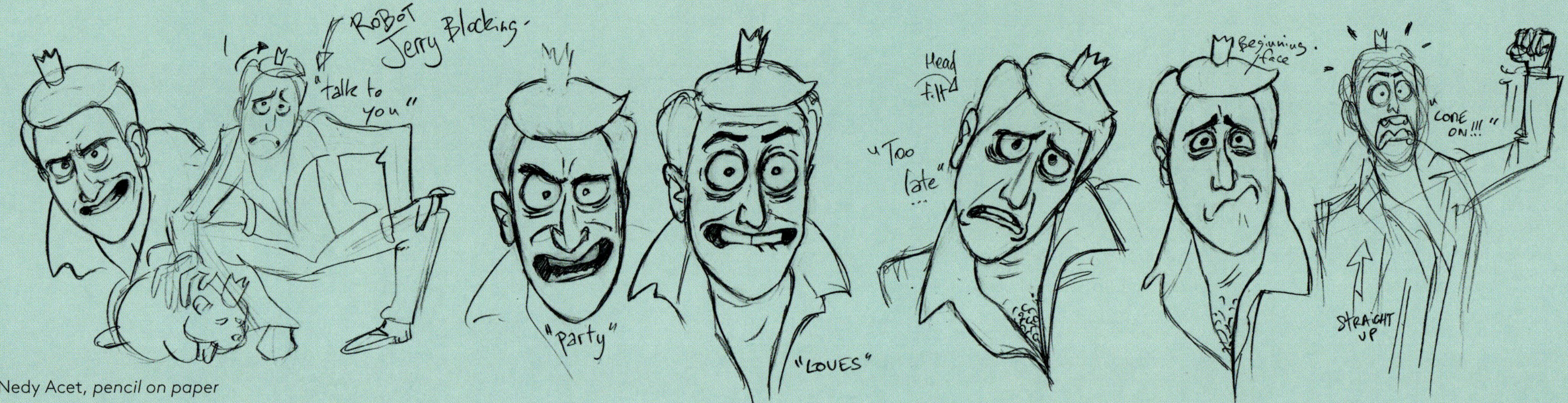

Nedy Acet, *pencil on paper*

Ke Yang, *digital*

Hye Sung Kim, *digital*

Ke Yang, *digital*

John Cody Kim, *ink and marker on paper*

SONIC TREE TERROR

Nira Liu, John Cody Kim, Vanessa Guvele, and Michael Fong, *digital*

This scene is an exciting challenge of weaving together Titus's personality and quirks, all while he inhabits an unfamiliar robotic body replica of Mayor Jerry. The challenge of capturing the nuance of a character acting inside of another character makes the performance of this scene standout and unique. All this is followed by a thrilling and physically complex performance of Titus desperately trying to regain his power. **Alon Winterstein, animation supervisor**

FACE ID
NOT RECOGNIZED

Kyle Jones, *digital*

Daniel López Muñoz, *digital*

John Cody Kim, *ink and marker on paper*

John Cody Kim, *ink and marker on paper*

Anna Scott, *digital*

Margaret Spencer, *ink and marker on paper*

Victor Navone, *digital*

Hye Sung Kim, *digital*

Hye Sung Kim, *digital*

John Cody Kim, *ink and marker on paper*

Ben Su, *digital*

Daniel López Muñoz, *digital*

FIRE BREAKOUT

Michael Fong, Vanessa Guvele, and Hannah Roman, *digital*

The fire scene symbolizes everything Mabel has fought for going up in flames. Mabel is desperate and alone, but her animal friends rescue her in time! I wanted the Pond Crew to feel heroic and awesome, so I drew them leaping over high flames to Mabel's rescue. Even after Mabel loses everything, her friends are there to pick her up when she needs them the most. **Vanessa Guvele, story artist**

Daniel López Muñoz, *digital*

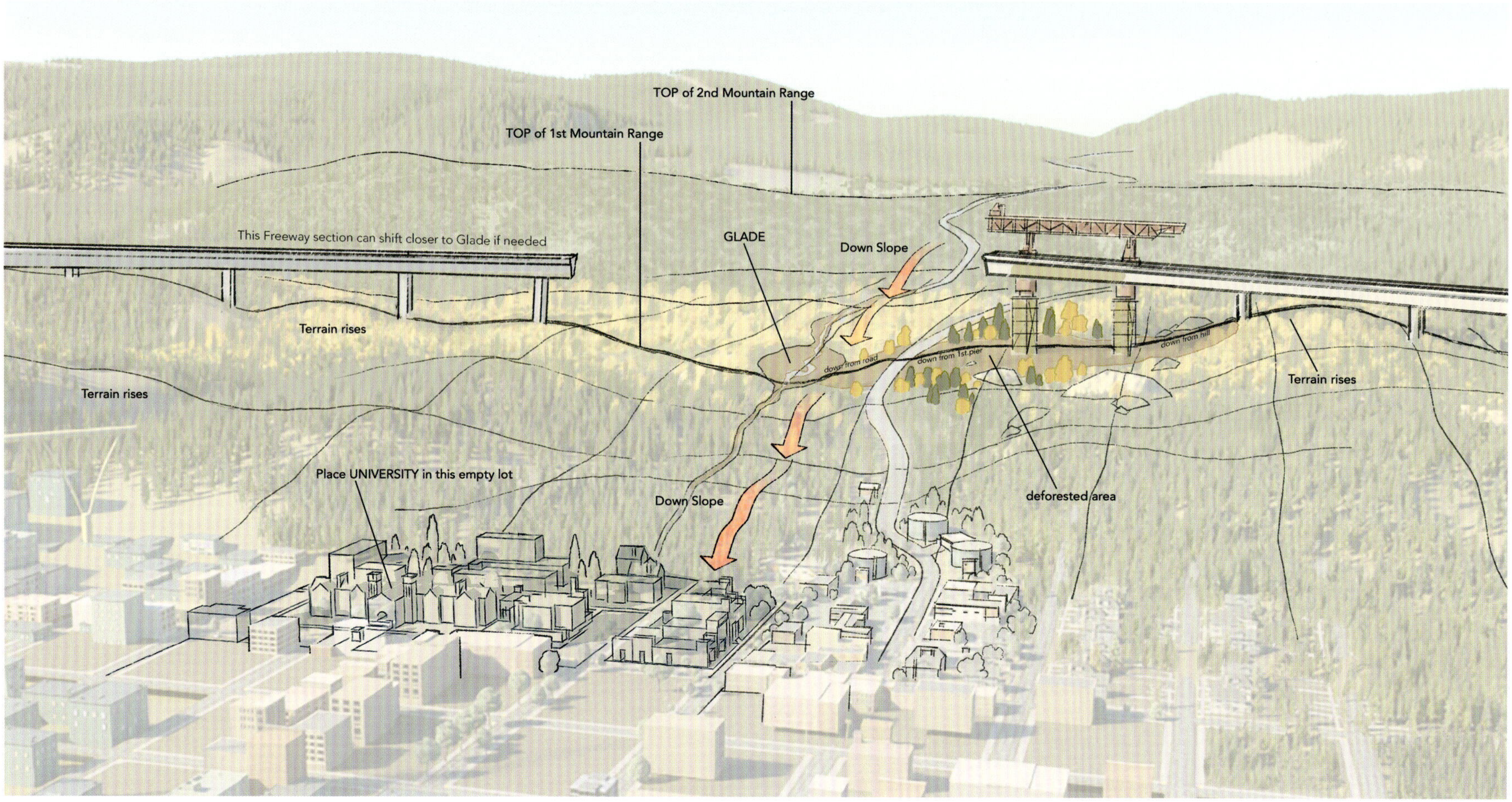

Daniel López Muñoz, *digital*

John Cody Kim, *ink on paper*

Daniel López Muñoz, *digital*

DESTROY THE DAM

Nira Liu, Jamie Baker, John Cody Kim, and Hannah Roman, *digital*

This sequence is all about everyone in the Pond Crew pitching in to avert disaster in the nick of time. That's also pretty much what it was like storyboarding this sequence! Every artist in the *Hoppers* story team had a hand in finishing this sequence. Pond Rules! **Jamie Baker, story artist**

Daniel López Muñoz, *digital*

In ecology, a *refugium* (plural: *refugia*) is a place where plants and animals can survive during unfavorable environmental conditions. These refugia can take many forms: caves during a thunderstorm, shady forests during a heat wave, or—as seen here—beaver wetlands during a wildfire. Though beavers are more commonly known as "nature's engineers" than "nature's firefighters," the idea of them protecting other species from spreading flames is more fact than fiction. Scientists have found that the wetlands beavers create are uniquely resistant to wildfire. On average, beaver wetlands burn three times less than river ecosystems without beavers, and approximately 90 percent of beaver wetlands serve as fire refugia—even during megafires. It is not uncommon to visit a beaver wetland after a fire and find all sorts of fish, amphibians, mammals, birds, and reptiles taking refuge there.

Dr. Emily Fairfax, assistant professor, University of Minnesota

Daniel López Muñoz, *digital*

Valerie Kao and Daniel López Muñoz, *digital*

Daniel López Muñoz, *digital*

Wesley Fuh, *digital*

Hye Sung Kim, *digital*

John Cody Kim, *ink on paper*

Valerie Kao, *digital*

John Cody Kim, *ink on paper*

Wesley Fuh, *digital*

Hye Sung Kim, *digital*

Colorscript

In nature, we can see the wide range of colors from literally everywhere, and we can also enjoy the beautiful harmony that those colors create with the natural light.

Hye Sung Kim, shading and lighting art director

THIS SPREAD Hye Sung Kim, *digital*

Out of Picture

Hello. I am the person who came up with a lot of the words in *Hoppers*. It took about three years.

A word is kind of like a picture but much easier to make. You don't need to have what we in the movie industry call "talent." You just press a few buttons on a keyboard with your soft, gentle fingertips. Then you hit the space bar. That's all it takes. Usually it's less than eight buttons.

Sometimes I feel a little silly that this is my job. Other times I feel drunk with power, because when you are a words person at an animation studio full of art people, your words are always getting converted into glorious, funny, mesmerizing pictures that you could never in a hundred billion years make yourself. All you have to do is type a sentence like "A bunch of seagulls dive into the ocean and pull out a shark." Then a dozen or so of the greatest artists in the entire industry have to spend all their time figuring out what that would even look like. They spend months visually manifesting a sentence that took about fifteen seconds to write. It probably would have gone even faster if I hadn't been typing with two fingers because I was using the rest of my fingers to eat a breakfast taco.

At this point you may be asking, "Jesse, how could your job possibly have taken three years to do?" I hear this question from lots of people, most notably my wife, who managed to have two different children during the time that I was writing most (but not all) of the words of *Hoppers*.

The answer is that Pixar likes to spend a lot of time iterating different versions of its movies. So for every page of words that made it into the movie, I've written dozens of pages that didn't. Words with sentences like "George has a really cool bachelor pad, from when he wasn't king yet." Or "Right now this is a movie about penguins and a helicopter."

And those sentences, too, get turned into pictures by the genius artists who work here. We sit around and look at them and often—even though the pictures are delightful—we know deep in our hearts that our movie probably wants to go in a different direction.

Madeline Sharafian, *digital*

Madeline Sharafian, *digital*

That's when I stand up and say, with breakfast taco crumbs spilling out of my mouth, "Don't worry, everyone. I'm going to go type a whole bunch more stuff for you to draw."

And the artists in the room let out a long, weary sigh and say, "Great."

I love my job.

Jesse Andrews, screenwriter

Melody Cisinski, *digital*

Madeline Sharafian, *digital*

John Cody Kim, *digital*

Daniel Chong, *digital*

Daniel Chong, *ink and marker on paper*

John Cody Kim, *ink on paper*

Madeline Sharafian, *digital*

John Cody Kim, *digital*

John Cody Kim, *digital*

Daniel Chong, *digital*

Daniel Chong, *digital*

mabel's journey brings her closer to an array of animal creatures she has only dreamed about.

even on the run, King george is a thoughtful leader.

Wesley Fuh, *digital*

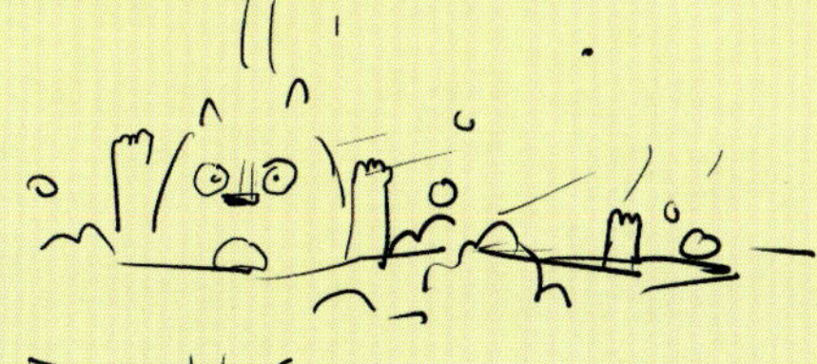

crumble

CRUSTACEAN KING

Madeline Sharafian, *digital*

WORM KING

Margaret Spencer, *digital*

Daniel Chong, *digital*

Daniel Chong, *digital*

Ke Yang, *digital*

Madeline Sharafian, *digital*

We had a lot of fun coming up with scientists who would have been zany enough to join Dr. Sam in her hopping crusade. We drew inspiration from puppet fabricators, Imagineers, even our own classmates at film school! We wanted a group that felt passionate but uniquely weird, people who eventually you'd root for Mabel to befriend. A few of my favorites were Candace, who would hop into a moose and obsess over getting into character a little too much, and Trigger, who hopped into a coyote but had a pretty robotic personality to begin with.

Madeline Sharafian, additional story supervisor

Ke Yang, *digital*

Madeline Sharafian, *digital*

Madeline Sharafian, *digital*

John Cody Kim, *digital*

John Cody Kim, *digital*

Daniel Chong, *digital*

Sylvain Marc, *digital*

Sylvain Marc, *digital*

In the movie, George tells Mabel the story of his banishment before returning to be king. And so we naturally figured if Mabel and George were on the run, the safest place might be George's old banishment spot (a.k.a. his bachelor pad). Part man cave, part hoarder's paradise, this abandoned beaver lodge is where George formed who he became in his early years. We also filled it with human items he collected, which built George's interest and empathy for humans. Ultimately, though, we had to cut it for time.

Daniel Chong, director

John Cody Kim, *digital*

In an early version of the film, George was banished to this motel swimming pool by the rest of the council. George was at his lowest point here in the pool, and Mabel was searching for him to make amends. Banishment was the worst thing that could happen to a beaver, so we wanted to make sure the location felt secluded and desolate. While this scene ultimately didn't stay in the film, it helped shape the scene "Now What?" where George and Mabel connect after conflict.

Lucy Laliberte, production manager

Anna Scott, *digital*

Anna Scott, *digital*

Anna Scott, *digital*

Charles Choo, *digital*

Madeline Sharafian, *digital*

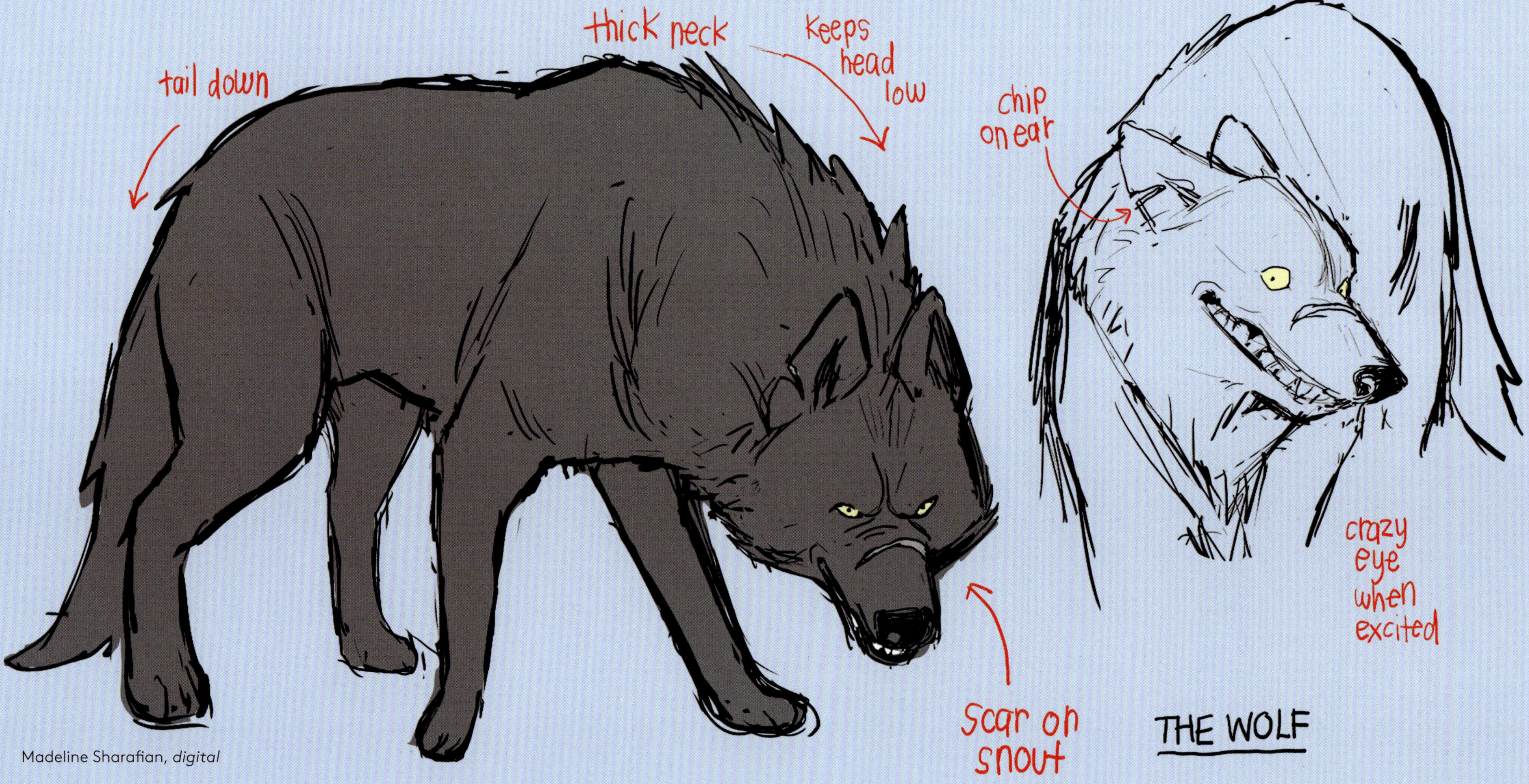

tail down
thick neck
Keeps head low
chip on ear
crazy eye when excited
Scar on snout
THE WOLF

Madeline Sharafian, *digital*

Daniel Chong, *digital*

There's a convention in a lot of spy movies when the heroes are on the run: The bad guys call a bunch of sleeper agent assassins to take them out. We thought this would be hilarious in the animal world, with the council calling a bunch of apex predators from all over. In the end we had to condense this down to just one, but really it could've been any of these guys. My favorite assassin (though not really an apex predator) was a little poison frog that breaks out of a zoo when called.

Daniel Chong, director

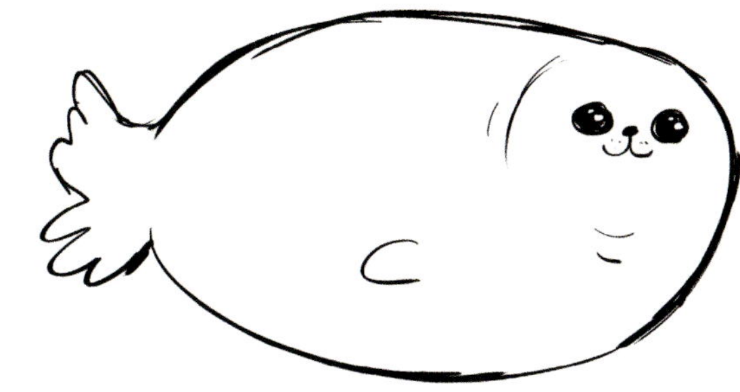

Madeline Sharafian, *digital*

Wesley Fuh, *digital*

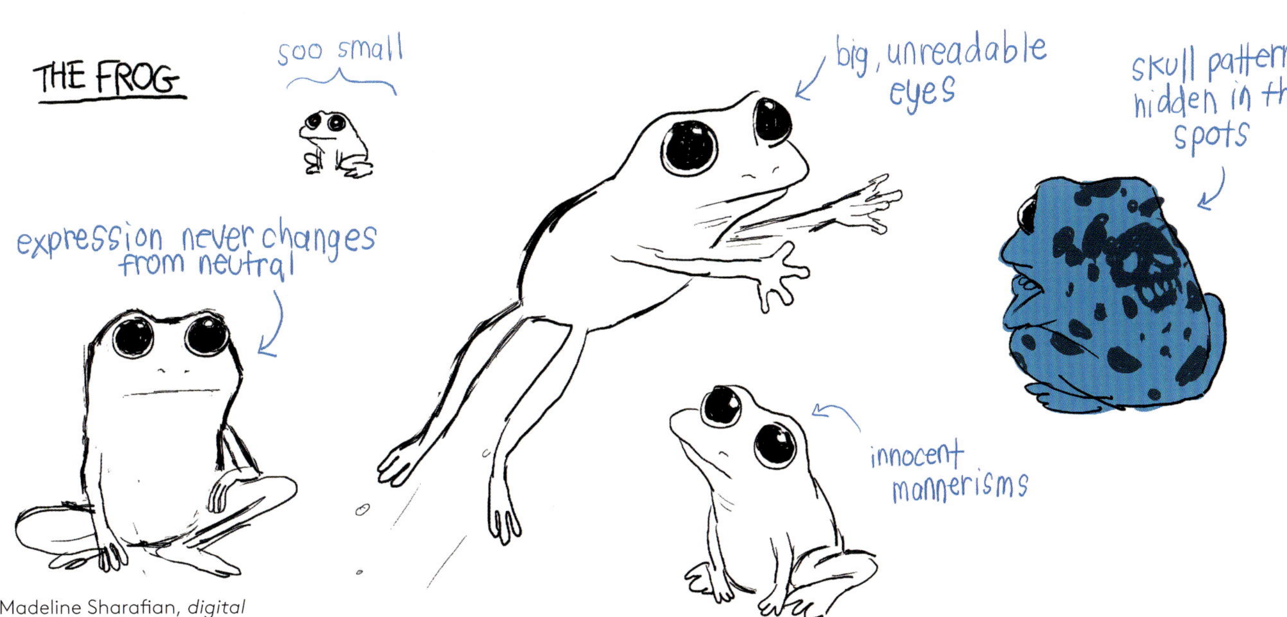

Madeline Sharafian, *digital*

Acknowledgments

We are humbled that *Hoppers* is Pixar's thirtieth film in the year of its fortieth anniversary as a studio. It has been our aspiration to make a classic Pixar film worthy of this milestone—a film with humor and heart that tells us how to live as humans, but this time alongside animals within the natural world.

The world of *Hoppers* operates on a set of principles called Pond Rules, which describe a way of living in community that promotes consideration and cooperation, especially during times of stress. And these were in play as much during the making of this film as they are in the story we told. Since making a film is very difficult and requires a great deal of consideration and cooperation, in some ways, we lived the story we were telling.

DON'T BE A STRANGER

Let's make introductions. First and foremost, this world has sprung from the vivid imagination of Daniel Chong, whose playful sensibility is matched only by his kindness and generosity as a creator. But it couldn't have come to fruition without production designer Bryn Imagire, who designed a world that gives you the *feeling* of being in nature without being a photoreal imitation of nature, a world that marries the stylized character designs with the environments they inhabit.

Bryn oversaw her Art team with managers Pauline Chu and Jessica Heidt, as well as coordinator Marina Capizzi. We are immensely grateful for the fine work of art directors Anna Scott, Daniel Holland, and Hye Sung Park, who headed up the effort to design an enormous and complex natural world. They were supported by a fantastic core team of artists: Valerie Kao, Daniel López Muñoz, Ke Yang, Lauren Kawahara, Kaleb Rice, Philip Metschan, Carlos Felipe León, Jacy Zuckerbrow, Bert Berry, Laura Phillips, Annlyn Huang, Asha Farmer, Sandeep Menon, Ellen Moon Lee, Andy Jimenez, Greg Dykstra, and Jerome Ranft. We also want to acknowledge the truly inspirational work done by Francesca Fedele, Kerascoët, Keiko Murayama, Airi Pan, Sylvain Marc, Yogin, Louie Zong, Meghan Sasaki, and Gaston Ugarte.

WHEN YOU GOTTA EAT, EAT

When you gotta take care of yourself, take care of yourself. Health care and self-care include mental health. And laughter is the best medicine. So we laughed, but we also appreciated that people needed a space where they felt safe to do their best work. Production of this film spanned the COVID-19 global pandemic and the shift of work from office to home to hybrid and back again to the office. We took care of one another during all these transitions, and it became woven into the fabric of this film.

Now back to the introductions. The design of this world sprang from the storytelling. In the beginning, there were Daniel's sketches, and then there was writing.

Writing inspired storyboarding, and storyboarding inspired writing in an especially circular relationship on this team. Our brilliant and hilarious screenwriter Jesse Andrews would sit with director Daniel Chong, our amazing story supervisors John Cody Kim and Madeline Sharafian, and phenomenal lead story artists Hannah Roman and Margaret Spencer, and the group would collaborate on storytelling, which often allowed visual gags to drive the narrative as much as writing would drive the storyboarding. And all this came together in the editing suite with the collaboration of editor Axel Geddes.

We were so grateful to have a wonderfully gifted core Story team: Michael Fong, Vanessa Guvele, Jamie Baker, Wesley Fuh, Nira Liu, and Tessa Abrams, along with early days help from Lorenzo Fresta. And thanks also go to story managers Samantha Gruwell and Max Sachar, along with coordinators Kristina Truong, Gemma Trezza, and Jarred Gregory-Grimes.

WE'RE ALL IN THIS TOGETHER

Our story is rooted in the beauty of the natural world, and especially the beaver world. Beavers are a keystone species whose presence creates an environment that is beneficial to all the life around them. We could learn a thing or two from them. So it was essential to do them justice. We did our best to balance factual details with the fantastic premise of our story. All things beavers were learned at the feet of the great Emily Fairfax, PhD, who led our Art team into an actual beaver habitat, where they got as up close and personal as is possible with wild beavers, in the water and in the mud, to ensure we got things right. We are also grateful to George Bumann, our guide on an in-depth visit to Yellowstone National Park exploring the intelligence of animals; George helped us appreciate what it feels like to be an animal in the animal world, and showed us how terribly disruptive and destructive we noisy humans can be in their environment. Thank you to Megan Alderson for bringing all the development research together and helping us connect with these essential resources. We owe a huge debt of gratitude to former Pixar librarian and amateur naturalist Carol Wing, whose love for animals and the natural world is part of the very foundation of our movie. And I would be remiss if I didn't also acknowledge how much our animation and technical artists brought to the realization of the vision laid out in this book. So much nuance and expressive detail was added by each artist who worked on the film.

WORK IS THE PARTY!

Like the beavers in our movie, we worked and worked some more, but always had fun, even when it was hard. Executive producer Pete Docter was with us on this journey from the very first pitch. His love for this concept has helped us keep the faith during the most challenging days. Over the years of production, we have also benefited from the wisdom of executive producers Peter Sohn, Kiri Hart, Domee Shi, and Lee Unkrich, along with associate executive producer Rosana Sullivan. Their enthusiastic support and guidance kept us on track as they demonstrated an ability to help us preserve what was working while peeling away to get to the kernel of the story we were trying to tell.

We are grateful for the support of the Pixar executives who believed in us and this story: Jim Morris, Jonas Rivera, Katherine Sarafian, Lindsey Collins, Steve May, Jim Kennedy, Chris Kaiser, Jonathan Garson, Reema Batnagar, and Jessie Schroeder.

Madeline Sharafian, *digital*

Nobody can get anything done without the help of Feature Relations and Legal, so immense gratitude to Melissa Bernabei, Laura Finnell, Jody Weinberg, Serena Martinez Dettman, John Lomazzi, and Elliot Simons.

And for this book in particular, the biggest thank-you of all for the expert stewardship of our Pixar and Disney Publishing team, Jenny Spring and Alberto Manquero, and from Chronicle Books, thanks to Liam Flanagan, Neil Egan, Maddy Wong, Juliette Capra, Tera Killip, Perry Crowe, and Beth Weber.

Making a film creates an intimate bond for an intense period of time, and I am so grateful for the warmth, camaraderie, and good humor of our *Hoppers* Production leadership team: Michael Warch, Beth Albright, and Lucy Laliberte, as well as Amy Ellenwood, Bryan Read, Christine Jiang, and Rob Cassie. They really did make work the party!

Thank you to our families for your patience and forgiveness for the many hours we've neglected you over all these many years. Your love and support literally sustain us and are part of the fabric of this story.

And to the entire *Hoppers* crew, our real-life Pond Crew, in addition to your immense skill and talent, thank you for bringing joy and laughter to our work on this film every single day, and thereby into this movie and out into the world. Because we're all in this together.

POND RULES!

Nicole Paradis Grindle, producer

Hye Sung Kim, *digital*

HOPPING